The

Oldest Dead

White European

Males

BY BERNARD KNOX

Oedipus at Thebes: Sophocles' Tragic Hero and His Time
Oedipus the King
The Heroic Temper: Studies in Sophoclean Tragedy
Word and Action: Essays on the Ancient Theater
Essays Ancient and Modern
The Cambridge History of Classical Literature, volume 1, Greece
(coeditor and contributor)
The Norton Book of Classical Literature (editor)
The Norton Anthology of World Masterpieces (coeditor)

THE

OLDEST DEAD

WHITE EUROPEAN

MALES

and Other Reflections on the Classics

BERNARD KNOX

W · W · *Norton & Company* · *New York* · *London*

The text of this book is composed in Sabon
with the display set in Centaur
Composition and manufacturing by
The Haddon Craftsmen, Inc.
Book design by Guenet Abraham

Library of Congress Cataloging-in-Publication Data

Knox, Bernard MacGregor Walker.
The oldest dead white European males and other reflections
on the classics / Bernard Knox.
p.   cm
Includes index.
Greek literature—History and criticism—Theory, etc.
2. Civilization, Western—Greek influences.
3. Literature, Modern—Greek influences.
4. Greece—Civilization.   I. Title.
PA3071.K58   1993
880.9′ 001—dc20   92-32689
ISBN 0-393-31233-X

SEAMUS HEANEY: Excerpt from *The Cure at Troy*. Copyright
© 1991 by Seamus Heaney. Reprinted by permission of
Farrar, Straus and Giroux, Inc. and Faber and Faber Ltd.
RICHMOND LATTIMORE: Excerpt from Aristophanes' *Frogs* in
Aristophanes: Four Comedies, edited by William
Arrowsmith. Copyright © 1961, 1962, 1964, 1967, 1969 by
William Arrowsmith. Reprinted by permission of University
of Michigan Press.
LOUIS MACNEICE: Excerpts from "Autumn Journal" from *The
Collected Poems of Louis MacNeice*, edited by E. R. Dodds.
Copyright © 1966 by the Estate of Louis MacNeice.
Reprinted by permission of Oxford University Press and
Faber and Faber Ltd.
DOUGLASS PARKER: Excerpt from Aristophanes' *Lysistrata* in
Aristophanes: Four Comedies, edited by William
Arrowsmith. Copyright © 1961, 1962, 1964, 1967, 1969 by
William Arrowsmith. Reprinted by permission of University
of Michigan Press.

W. W. Norton & Company, Inc.
500 Fifth Avenue, New York, N.Y. 10110

W. W. Norton & Company Ltd.
10 Coptic Street, London WC1A 1PU

5 6 7 8 9 0

For Bianca, as always

CONTENTS

FOREWORD

The three essays printed in this book were originally lectures delivered at different times and places: the first in Washington, D.C., as the 1992 Jefferson Lecture, sponsored by the National Endowment for the Humanities, the second at Yale University in 1981, as the inaugural lecture at the opening of the Whitney Humanities Center, and the third in 1988 at Muncie, Indiana, as one of the distinguished series of Provost's

Lectures offered by Ball State University. But they are all concerned, mainly or exclusively, with the same theme: the Greeks and the heritage they have handed down to our Western civilization.

This is today a controversial theme, as the deliberately provocative title of the first essay suggests. Advocates of multiculturalism and militant feminists, among others, have denounced the traditional canon of literature that has so long served as the educational base for Western societies, repudiating it not only as sexist and racist but even as the instrument of ideological *Gleichschaltung* used by a ruling class to impose conformity. At the heart of this so-called canon, its source and still after all these years its vital core, are the masterpieces of classical Greek literature: the epic poems of Homer; the tragedies of Aeschylus, Sophocles, and Euripides; the comedies of Aristophanes; the histories of Herodotus and Thucydides; the odes of Pindar and the remnants of the other lyric poets, Sappho their brightest star; and the dialogues of Plato.

The critics seem, at first sight, to have a case. The characteristic political unit of classical Greek society—the *polis,* or city-state—was very much a man's club; even in its most advanced form, Athenian democracy, it relegated its women to silence and anonymity. Racism in our sense was not a problem of the Greeks; their homogeneous population afforded no soil on which that weed could easily grow. But the Greeks did, as a result of the Persian Wars, create the influential idea of Europe as separate from and opposed to Asia, and they also credited themselves with a moral and intellectual superiority to the "barbarians" of the rest of the world, though it should be remembered that the word "barbarian" meant only that the unfortunate people in question could not speak Greek. Lastly, that menacing canon that looms so large in the imaginative rhetoric of the academic radicals was a Greek invention.

When in the third and second centuries B.C., after the great age of Greek literary achievement, the scholars and critics of the Alexandrian library set to work to establish the texts of the classical authors and equip them with commentaries, they also established select lists of the principal figures in each literary genre. Homer and Hesiod were singled out from the immense body of early epic poetry as the great masters. Among the lyric poets nine were nominated for immortality—Pindar, Bacchylides, Sappho, Anacreon, Stesichorus, Ibycus, Alcman, Alcaeus, and Simonides. The crowned heads of the tragic stage were Aeschylus, Sophocles, and Euripides and of the comic stage Aristophanes, Eupolis, and Cratinus. There were lists of the best historians and philosophers and also a list of the ten greatest Attic orators, Demosthenes prominent among them. Though "canon" is an ancient Greek word (it means a carpenter's rule), it was not the word the Alexandrian scholars used. It was first used in this sense in 1768 by the German scholar David Ruhnken (the one with whom the great English scholar Richard Porson claimed to have "got more drunken"). The Alexandrian term for the canonized authors was *hoi enkrithentes,* "the admitted" or "the included." The Romans expressed the idea with the word *classicus,* a term derived from their political institutions, meaning literally "belonging to the highest class of citizens."

These "canons" were of more than academic importance for a world in which book production was a laborious business of hand copying and the papyrus on which the works were written a fragile and perishable medium. Books not "admitted" were liable to disappear as copies were not renewed over the span of the years. In the final, desperate centuries of classical civilization, the years of civil wars and massive foreign invasions, the vast bulk of ancient Greek literature, including, to our everlasting loss, most of the work of the nine lyric poets, vanished. The last copies disintegrated or were burned in the sack of the cities that housed them. Only those works transferred to the more durable (and expensive) material of parchment could survive, and in what was now a Christian world the pagan authors preserved were those thought necessary for the schooling of the young—a restricted version of the original canon: Homer, Hesiod, Herodotus, Thucydides; seven tragedies each for Aeschylus and Sophocles, ten for Euripides; eleven comedies of Aristophanes; and, partly no doubt because of the influence of Neoplatonic philosophy on the Christian theologians, all of Plato, and much of his successor Aristotle.

Yet, canon or no canon, it is strange to find the classical Greeks today assailed as emblems of reactionary conservatism, of enforced conformity. For their role in the history of the West has always been innovative, sometimes indeed subversive, even revolutionary.

When new, relatively stable kingdoms emerged at last from the chaos of the destruction and dissolution of Roman imperial rule in western Europe, Greek texts and the ability to read them were a thing of the past; the language of the Catholic church and of what literary training schools and monasteries provided was Latin. The Greek classics were known only through their reflection in the literature of the Roman poets. Dante, writing his *Divina Commedia* in the first half of the fourteenth century, gave Homer a place of honor among the pagan poets in Limbo but would not have been able to read him even if a Greek text had been available; for that matter he could not even have read him in a Latin translation, for no such thing existed. Dante saw Plato there, too, sitting with Socrates among those who "look to and honor" Aristotle, "the master of those who know." This reversal of the relationship of the two philosophers (Aristotle was a student of Plato's at the Academy for twenty years) reflects the fact that Plato's writings were unknown in the West, while Aristotle's had been transplanted, from Arabic versions into Latin, in the twelfth and thirteenth centuries. They had a powerful influence on scholastic philosophy and Christian theology; Thomas Aquinas, for example, wrote commentaries on no fewer than eleven of Aristotle's treatises (among them the *Nichomachean Ethics,* the *Metaphysics,* and the *Politics*) and incorporated Aristotelian method and principle into his magisterial and authoritative *Summa theologica.*

In the years that followed, texts of the Greek originals and teachers of the language appeared in Italy, as scholars moved there from Byzantium, now under threat from the Ottoman Turks, who would eventually capture the city in 1453. Petrarch, of the generation after Dante, was a pioneer in the revival of interest in neglected Latin classics and the rediscoverer of manuscripts of forgotten texts, such as the correspondence of Cicero. But he never learned more than the rudiments of

Greek. He did, however, read and admire Plato in the
Latin translations that now appeared, and when he died
was engaged in writing notes on a new Latin translation
of Homer made by a Greek scholar. In 1396 the Byzantine scholar Manuel Chrysolaras was invited to Florence
to teach the ancient language, and in 1439 the Greek
Neoplatonic philosopher Gemistus Plethon made such
an impression on the court of Cosimo dei Medici that a
Platonic academy was set up in Florence to translate and
study the works of the man whom Petrarch had already
hailed, years before, as the "prince of philosophers."
This Platonism was one of the salient characteristics of
the new humanism that set it in sharp contrast with the
medieval scholastic and Aristotelian frame of mind;
when, in England, instruction in Greek was first offered
at Oxford in 1516, it was vociferously denounced by a
student body that took the name of Trojans; they feared,
and rightly, that the new Greek studies heralded the
abandonment of the whole medieval scholastic system.
In this respect as in others, the study of the newly discovered Greek classics was one of the key elements of the
Renaissance, that age of renewed intellectual and scientific inquiry, of exploration and colonization, the beginning of the process in which the old, stable civilizations
of Asia, Africa, and the Americas were confronted with
the dynamics of change introduced by the West.

Greek was the instrument of change and disturbance in the religious as well as in the cultural sphere. With the spread of the knowledge of the Greek language, scholars could now read the Gospels in the language of the original writers, without the mediation of Saint Jerome's Latin translation, the basic text of Catholic teaching. Lorenzo Valla, the first translator of Thucydides and Herodotus, even went so far, in 1444, as to publish a pamphlet listing the "mistakes" in Jerome's venerable text. Greek, as was to be expected, was a favorite study of the leaders of the Reformation; Martin Luther's close associate and intellectual spokesman Philip Melanchthon (a Greek translation of his real name, Schwarzerde, "Blackearth") was professor of Greek at Wittenberg, the university where young Hamlet made friends with Rosencrantz and Guildenstern.

All through the turbulent sixteenth and seventeenth centuries Greek studies continued to play the role of intellectual gadfly. Thomas Hobbes, for example, who has been called the father of modern analytic philosophy and whose *Leviathan* is one of the most radical and dark assessments of human nature and society, began his career with an English translation of Thucydides, whom he thought "the most politic historiographer that ever writ." In his old age (he was eighty-six) he published verse translations of the *Iliad* and *Odyssey*. One of his closest friends was the French Jesuit Gassendi, whose presentation of the atomic theory of Epicurus as a model for understanding the world of phenomena was to have immense influence on modern atomic theory and, through it, on all our lives. Even in Victorian England, where the Greek classics had been adopted by such figures as Arnold of Rugby and Jowett of Balliol as the core of an education for an imperial upper class, James Frazer, a Greek scholar and fellow of Trinity College Cambridge, published in 1890 his *Golden Bough,* which did almost as much damage to the Victorian religious worldview as Darwin's *Origin of Species.* Even more subversive of received ideas was the work of a professor of Greek at the University of Basel, Friedrich Nietzsche. And in 1900 Sigmund Freud, in his *Interpretation of Dreams,* announced one of the most sensational and disturbing theories ever propounded, in a passage which attempted to explain why Sophocles' play *Oedipus the King* can stir the emotions of a modern audience as deeply as it did those of the fifth-century Athenians.

All through the history of the West the Greeks have continued to spur innovation; the contact of the modern mind with the ancient has time and again resulted in a renewal or (Nietzsche's phrase) reversal of values. One might say of the Greeks what in Thucydides' *History* the Corinthians say of the Athenians: "You could sum them up by saying that they were born never to live in peace and quiet themselves and to prevent the rest of the world from doing so."

In other respects, too, the revisionist case lacks cogency. It is hard, for example, to think of a historical work that is more multicultural than that of Herodotus. As a background for the epic struggles between the Greeks and the Persian empire, he devotes one of his seven books to the history, culture, and religion of Egypt, an admiring assessment that gives the Egyptians more credit on some counts than they deserve, as well as providing us with full accounts of the customs and religion of the Lydians, Babylonians, Massagetae, Indians, Arabians, Scythians, Libyans, Thracians, and Paeonians; he also gives us a detailed history of the rise of the Persian mountaineers to control of their enormous land empire and the deliberations, actions, and personal lives of the Persian Great Kings Cyrus, Cambyses, Darius, and Xerxes. In fact one of the charges brought against him many centuries later by Plutarch in his essay *The Malice of Herodotus* is that he was *philobarbaros,* "too fond of foreigners." And though it is true that Athenian democracy allowed women no scope for public or political activity, Attic tragedy has given us a wealth of impressive female figures—Antigone, Electra, Medea, Hecuba, Clytemnestra—who still, on our screens and stages, in translation or modern adaptation, challenge us with disturbing visions of women's heroism and suffering.

The primacy of the Greeks in the canon of Western literature is neither an accident nor the result of a decision imposed by higher authority; it is simply a reflection of the intrinsic worth of the material, its sheer originality and brilliance. It was no academic ukase that made E. V. Rieu's Penguin translation of the *Odyssey* one of the great best-sellers of publishing history, and the film and stage directors who return obsessively to the masterpieces of the Greek theater are not driven by the ideological imperatives of a ruling class.

As for the multicultural curriculum that is the ideal of today's academic radicals, there can be no valid objection to the inclusion of new material that gives the student a wider view. But that new material will have to compete with the old, and if it is not up to the same high level it will sooner or later be rejected with disdain by the students themselves; only a totalitarian regime can enforce the continued study of second-rate texts or outworn philosophies. As long as the thoroughly Greek idea of competition is allowed free play, there is no need to worry about the future place of the Greeks in the curriculum; even if they are temporarily shunted aside in some places, they will make their way back; indeed, they may even win a wider audience as rejected texts. They have stood the test of time, more than two thousand years of it, and have become a basic element of our character, of our nature. And, as the Roman poet Horace remarked, you may toss nature out with a pitchfork, but it will still come running back in.

THE

OLDEST DEAD

WHITE EUROPEAN

MALES

One

THE OLDEST DEAD WHITE
EUROPEAN MALES

I

The species known as DWEM, which has only recently been isolated and identified, is already the focus of intense controversy. As usually happens to newly discovered species, it is even being broken down into subspecies—DWAM, for example, the title of a course recently offered at a university, with readings presumably in such writers as Thoreau, Emerson, and Mark

Twain, not to mention Thomas Jefferson of Virginia. I propose to discuss, however, the European type and, in particular, its first appearance on the face of the planet.

My specimens are certainly dead; in fact they have been in that condition longer than any other members of the species—for more than twenty-five hundred years. In spite of recent suggestions that they came originally from Ethiopia, it is clear, from their artistic representations of their own and other races, that they were undoubtedly white or, to be exact, a sort of Mediterranean olive color. They invented the idea and gave us the name of Europe, fixing its imagined frontier at the long sea passage between the Black Sea and the Mediterranean, waters that Xerxes, the Great King of the Persians, crossed, Herodotus tells us, on his way from Asia to Europe. And they created a form of society in which, for all practical purposes (which for them were war, politics, litigation, and competitive athletics), women played no part whatsoever. I am speaking, of course, about the ancient Greeks, particularly those of the eighth through the fourth centuries before the birth of Christ.

Their assignment to the DWEM category is one of the accomplishments of modern multicultural and radical feminist criticism; it is a declaration of their irrelevance. Previous ages, however, spoke of them in very different terms. "We are all Greeks," wrote Percy Bysshe Shelley in 1822; "our laws, our literature, our religion, our arts, have their roots in Greece." There is some exaggeration here, especially in the matter of the Christian religion, which has deeper and wider roots in Hebrew Palestine than in Neoplatonic philosophy; Shelley, who had been expelled from Oxford for writing and circulating a pamphlet entitled *The Necessity of Atheism,* was not exactly an expert in this field. But by 1865 this identification with the ancient Greeks had advanced so far that, as Frank Turner puts it in his fascinating book *The Greek Heritage in Victorian Britain,* "the major commentator on Homer as well as a major translator of the poet, the chief critic and historian of Greek literature, the most significant political historians of Greece and the authors of the then most extensive commentaries on Greek philosophy either were or had recently been members of the House of Commons or the House of Lords." The ancient Greeks were not seen just as roots but as fully formed models of Victorian moral and intellectual culture. George Grote, the "intellectual and tactical leader of the philosophic radicals in the House of Commons," was the author of the classic *History of Greece,* in which the Athenian assembly bears a startling resemblance to the House of Commons, with Pericles as prime minister and his opponent Thucydides son of Melesias as leader of Her Majesty's loyal opposition. And William Ewart Gladstone, in the intervals of serv-

ing as president of the Board of Trade, colonial secre-
tary, chancellor of the exchequer, and four terms as
prime minister, found time to write a series of books,
one of them in three volumes, on Homer, in which he
tried to prove that the Greeks, like the Jews, were a
chosen people, entrusted by God with "no small share of
those treasures of which the Semitic family of Abraham
were to be the appointed guardians, on behalf of mankind, until the fullness of time should come." The Victorians appropriated the ancient Greeks, imagined them
as contemporaries, and used their writings as weapons
in their own ideological wars. If they had been attuned
to modern advertising techniques, they might have re-
versed Shelley's claim and launched the slogan GREEKS
"я" US.

There was a reaction, of course. Scholars such as Jane
Harrison, Sir James Frazer, and Andrew Lang, drawing
on the rather unreliable anthropological material available to them at the time—unreliable because most of it
had been compiled by Christian missionaries who, like
Gladstone, tried to detect premonitions of Christianity
in what they regarded as the aberrations of the primitive
mind—painted a very different picture of the religious

ideas and practices of the Greeks. And historians developed a more acerbic view of the realities of Athenian democratic infighting—the ostracism of Aristides the Just, the exile of Themistocles, who had saved Athens in the Persian War, the assassination of Ephialtes, the reformist colleague of Pericles, the temporary overthrow of the democracy by an oligarchic coup d'état in 411 B.C., and the reign of terror of the Thirty Tyrants, backed by victorious Spartan troops, in 404. And in 1938, Louis MacNeice, who was a professor of Greek at the University of Birmingham as well as, next to Auden, the finest poet of his generation, bade a melancholy farewell to the glory that was Greece in his poem "Autumn Journal." Contemplating the prospect of once more acting, to use his own phrase, as "impresario of the ancient Greeks," he sketches an ironic picture of the professor preparing his lectures on Greek civilization.

The Glory that was Greece: put it in a syllabus, grade it
  Page by page
To train the mind or even to point a moral
  For the present age:
Models of logic and lucidity, dignity, sanity,
  The golden mean between opposing ills. . . .

But then he suddenly turns his back on this familiar and comfortable prospect:

> *But I can do nothing so useful or so simple;*
>   *These dead are dead*
> *And when I should remember the paragons of Hellas*
>   *I think instead*
> *Of the crooks, the adventurers, the opportunists,*
>   *The careless athletes and the fancy boys,*
> *The hair-splitters, the pedants, the hard-boiled sceptics*
>   *And the Agora and the noise*
> *Of the demagogues and the quacks; and the women*
>   *pouring*
>   *Libations over graves*
> *And the trimmers at Delphi and the dummies at Sparta*
>   *and lastly*
>   *I think of the slaves.*
>
> *And how one can imagine oneself among them*
>   *I do not know;*
> *It was all so unimaginably different*
>   *And all so long ago.*

The Roman word for "poet," *vates,* also meant "inspired prophet," and in these lines MacNeice, as poets so often do, unconsciously anticipates future developments. For in the fifty or so years since he wrote them, classical scholars have concentrated their attention on the dark underside of what the Victorians hailed as the Greek Miracle. There is hardly an aspect of ancient Greek civilization that has not been relentlessly explored, analyzed, and exposed in its strangeness, its "otherness," to use a once fashionable term borrowed from the French existentialists, by scholars armed with the insights and methods of anthropology, sociology, psychology, psychoanalysis, structuralism, deconstruction, narratology, semiotics, and all the other proliferating weapons of the modern intellectual armory. If the Victorian vision of Greece could be summed up in the slogan GREEKS "я" US, the modern critics could retort GREEKS "я" THEM, or rather, as some of them have, GREEKS "я" DWEM.

■ ■ ■

II

The results, of course, have been mixed. It might be said of the new approaches to Greek culture and literature what Sophocles in a famous choral ode of the *Antigone* said of humankind in general: "Equipped with the ingenuity of its techniques, a thing subtle beyond expectation, it makes its way sometimes to bad, sometimes to good." I cannot hope to deal with every aspect of the vast reevaluation of the Greek heritage that has been under way for the last fifty years; I shall confine my remarks to four topics: anthropology, psychology, slavery, and women.

One thing is certain: the strangeness, the "otherness" certainly exists; many of the normal, routine practices of the ancient Greeks seem to us not just strange but positively bizarre. One of the most common occurrences in any Greek epic text, for example, is a sacrifice. "Sacrifice," for us, is a blandly metaphorical word; we talk of a "sacrifice play" in team sports, or, more seriously, in the old formulas of the Christian communion service, "we offer and present unto thee, O Lord, ourselves, our souls and bodies, to be a reasonable, holy, and living sacrifice unto thee. . . ." And if we do think of sacrifice as a real ceremony, we are apt to see it in the romantic aura of John Keats's "Ode on a Grecian Urn":

> *Who are these coming to the sacrifice?*
>   *To what green altar, O mysterious priest,*
> *Lead'st thou that heifer lowing at the skies,*
>   *And all her silken flanks with garlands dressed?*

Keats stops right there; his urn didn't show what happened next. But Homer, more than once, gives us the full scenario. As the victim, a domestic animal, makes its way toward the rough stone altar (it may not be coerced), the presiding sacrificer cuts a tuft of hair from its head and throws it onto the fire that has been lit well in advance; he also scatters barley meal over the animal. Another ministrant swiftly brings an axe down on the animal's neck, cutting the tendons, and the women who are present raise their ritual shriek—*ololuge* is the Greek onomatopoeic word for it. Another celebrant pulls back the animal's head and cuts its throat; the blood is caught in a bowl and splashed on the altar. The carcass is now hacked apart; the tough (and valuable) hide, ripped off and set aside. The thigh bones are stripped of flesh, wrapped in layers of fat, and decorated with small pieces of meat from the edible parts of the victim; this is the portion of the gods, and as it is thrown on the fire the thick bluish smoke goes up toward their dwelling place in the clouds. Meanwhile, wine for the gods is poured out on the ground. The liver and heart of the animal are toasted on the fire and eaten, as the serious business of roasting the flesh proper begins. And all this hard and bloody work takes place in the glaring Aegean sun; the air is heavy with the odors of sweat, blood, burning fat, and the inedible offal of the animal that has been thrown away. And the flies—Homer speaks of them elsewhere as swarming round the milk pails in peacetime and, in a more sinister context, as feeding on the wounds of a dead warrior—the flies must have been there in swarms, covering the raw meat, stinging the butchers at their work. It is not like anything we know, but for Homer's audience it is routine, and always described in the same formulaic language; it is normal, on a par with the launching of a boat or the arming—or the death—of a warrior. And all this ritual bloodletting and butchery is not only the preliminary to a feast; it is also an act of worship of the Olympian gods.

For us, however, it is a puzzle: an elaborate pattern of behavior that seems at once naive—in its offering to the gods of the bones and fat decorated with some token tidbits of the edible meat—and sophisticated—in the careful ritualization that blunts the shock of the animal's violent death and through its pretense that the victim is willing tries to absolve the celebrants of any feeling of guilt. It is the kind of puzzle that anthropologists studying tribal customs in undeveloped countries are often faced with, and much of the best modern work on Greek culture has in fact been based on an anthropological approach to the problems it presents.

As early as 1724 a French Jesuit, Joseph Lafitau, who had lived in Canada among the Indians, published a book in which he made the remarkable claim that though he had learned from classic authors many things that helped him understand the people he refers to as "savages," the reverse was also true: "the customs of the Savages afforded me illumination the more easily to understand and explain several matters to be found in ancient authors." This passage is cited by Pierre Vidal-Naquet, one of a brilliant group of French cultural historians who have, in recent years, used the insights and techniques of modern anthropology to investigate the religious, moral, and political mentality of the ancient Greeks. Louis Gernet, little known in his lifetime, became famous after his student Jean-Pierre Vernant published a collection of his articles under the title *Anthropologie de la Grèce antique*. Vernant himself, especially concerned with what he calls *psychologie his-*

torique, "the history of the inner man," has given us a
wealth of fresh and illuminating perspectives on Greek
mythology, thought, religion, art, and literature, with a
special emphasis on tragedy. Some of his many books
have been works of collaboration: with Marcel Detienne, whose special field is religion and whose book
Les Jardins d'Adonis is the only successful and rewarding application of the methods of Lévi-Strauss to Greek
mythology; and with Vidal-Naquet, a historian who
concerns himself with *formes de pensée, formes de so-
ciété,* whose brilliant essays on ancient Greek politics,
society, and literature draw strength and depth from his
political engagement in the controversial issues of his
own time—the war in Algeria, the Holocaust—and his
sense of the vast perspectives, *la longue durée,* of history
(he recently served as editor of the remarkable *Atlas
Historique,* a history of the human race, from its prehis-
tory to 1987, that makes inspired use of creative cartog-
raphy and graphs).

The problem posed by the rites of sacrifice is, of
course, one of the principal concerns of these investiga-
tors—one of the many collaborative volumes issuing
from their circle bears the evocative title *La Cuisine du
sacrifice grec*—and it is also the focus of an extraordinary book by Walter Burkert that in its title has added to
the already existing classifications of humankind—

Homo erectus, Homo habilis, Homo sapiens, Homo sapiens sapiens, etc.—a new one: *Homo necans,* man the killer, the sacrificer. Developing the theories of the Swiss folklorist Karl Meuli, Burkert traces the sacrificial ritual back to the preagricultural hunters, who, by their preservation of its hide, skull, and thigh bones, mimed a symbolic reconstitution of the slaughtered wild beast in a ceremony that absolved them from responsibility for its death—the "comedy of innocence"—and served as a magical deterrent to the extinction of the hunted animal's species. When, in the agricultural phase, the victim was a domestic animal, the comedy of innocence, the pretense that the animal was a willing victim, became even more necessary. Burkert develops his thesis with immense learning and a probing analysis, directing new insights drawn from his thesis on every aspect of Greek ritual and myth.

III

One of the principal concerns of the Paris circle, the history of the inner man, was also the subject of an influential German book, Bruno Snell's *Entdeckung des*

Geistes, translated as *The Discovery of the Mind.* But unlike the theories of the Parisians, which, however far they may range in speculation, are always impressive and suggestive even when they cannot be fully accepted, Snell's thesis about the early Greek mind, specifically that of Homer, is fundamentally unsound. It is that the discovery of the mind is an achievement of post-Homeric Greece, that in Homer's poems we are in a world that has not yet conceived the idea of the individual consciousness, of the personality.

As might have been expected from the organizer of one of the most useful tools for research in the Homeric texts, a lexicon of early Greek epic language, Snell's method is strictly philological. He points out that there is no word in the Homeric vocabulary for the spiritual or intellectual organ that we call "the soul" or "consciousness." There is, of course, the word *psyche,* but it is used only of whatever it is that leaves the body with the advent of death. For the emotional and intellectual functions of the living man Homeric language offers a plurality of organs: the *thymos,* seat of violent passions, especially anger; the *phrenes,* seat of rational consideration and corresponding intention to act; *noos,* the organ of thought, of reflection, not connected with action or intention. And the word *phrenes,* which locates the rational faculty in the human body, does not mean, as we would expect, the brain; it means the diaphragm, the midriff.

Snell also claims that the Homeric language has no word for "body" either, except the word *soma,* which, as the ancient commentators pointed out, is used only of the dead body. The living body is thought of not as a unity but as a collection of separate limbs—arms, legs, torso, head—just as the consciousness appears not as a central entity but as the separate realms of *thymos, phrenes,* and *noos.* All this, taken together with the frequency of expressions that attribute human action to divine intervention, seems to him to rule out for Homeric man the existence of a personal self in any sense we can understand. Snell's conclusion is disconcerting. "As a further consequence," he sums up, "it appears that in the early period the 'character' of an individual is not yet recognized.... There is no denying that the great heroes . . . are drawn in firm outline and yet the reactions of Achilles, however grand and magnificent, are not explicitly presented in their volitional or intellectual form as character, i.e. as individual intellect and individual soul."

His case has one obvious weakness; it is an argument from silence, always a dangerous argument, especially so when applied to two long poems which we know are only a fragment of what once existed in this epic genre.

He is conscious of this weakness and tries to reinforce his position. "Through Homer," he writes, "we have come to know early European thought in poems of such length that we need not hesitate to draw our conclusions, if necessary, *ex silentio*. If some things do not occur in Homer though our modern mentality would lead us to expect them, we are entitled to assume that he had no knowledge of them."

But this rests on a false assumption, the assumption that the language of the epic poems is the language of Homeric society. It was not, of course, the language of Homeric society (whatever that phrase may mean) or of any society that ever existed; it was a language spoken by neither gods nor men, but one devised for epic song, full of ennobling archaisms and every word and form amenable to the prosodic demands of the epic hexameter line. One scholar (an American this time) has indeed gone so far as to argue that the Mycenean kings transmitted their mobilization orders in epic hexameter and that pilots used the same medium to pass on sailing directions, but this picture of epic verse as a functional means of everyday communication (which Snell needs in order for his argument from silence to be taken seriously) is a fantasy. Suppose a soldier made some smart rejoinder to the mobilization order, what would the officer of the day have said to him? Certainly not what

Homeric characters say to each other in such circumstances: *poion se epos phugen herkos odonton,* "What kind of word has escaped the stockade of your teeth?" There must have been some snappy Mycenean equivalent of "At ease, soldier!" and the chances are small that it would have fitted the metrical pattern of the hexameter line.

In any case, quite apart from the thoroughly compromised nature of the sample—the artificial language of epic verse—the lexical method itself, with its assumption that lack of a descriptive term argues the absence of the phenomenon for which there is no name, is a snare and a delusion. English, for example,—and I am not talking about twenty-seven thousand lines of early English verse, but about the whole range of spoken and written English from Chaucer to, say, Norman Mailer—has no word for that momentary self-congratulatory glow of satisfaction, immediately repressed, which is provoked by the news of the misfortunes of our friends—the reaction "Better him than me" or "It's about time he learned the facts of life." When we want to describe this emotion we have to fall back on a German word, *Schadenfreude.* It is to be hoped that no future student of *Geistesgeschichte* will announce, on this basis, that this ignoble emotion was never experienced by people who grew up speaking English—or French or, for that matter, Italian. English propagandists in the First World War made much of this fact and suggested that only the Huns had such base feelings. They kept silent about the fact that the classical Greeks, whom they had all been taught to admire by Dr. Jowett of Balliol, had a very expressive word for it: *epichairekakia*, "rejoicing over calamities." It is to be found in the *Nichomachean Ethics* of Aristotle, a text through which most Oxford men had been taken at a slow pace. Our researcher, however, had better look beyond the absence of such a word from the English and the French dictionaries. In the first edition of his *Reflexions morales*, published in 1665, the duc de La Rochefoucauld printed under the number 99 the following maxim:

> *Dans l'adversité de nos meilleurs amis nous trouvons toujours quelque chose qui ne nous déplaît pas.*
>
> (In the adversities of our best friends we always find something which is not displeasing to us.)

La Rochefoucauld suppressed this scandalous thought in all succeeding editions of his famous maxims, but Dean Swift, in Dublin, had read the first edition and presented the idea, in his own fashion, to the English-speaking public:

> *Wise Rochefoucauld a maxim writ*
> *Made up of malice, truth and wit. . . .*
> *He says: "Whenever Fortune sends*
> *Disaster to our dearest friends*
> *Although we outwardly may grieve*
> *We oft are laughing in our sleeve."*
> *And when I think upon't this minute*
> *I fancy there is something in it.*

But the flaws in the argument from silence are even more serious than at first appears. The silence is far from perfect. There is in fact a Homeric word for the body as a unit, *demas,* a word which Snell dismisses hurriedly on quite inadmissible technical grounds. And there are many passages in the poems that suggest a Homeric conception of the unified individual personality. There is above all the hero's name, the name he proudly bears and proclaims on all occasions, whether exulting over a fallen enemy or claiming his share of glory, that name

Odysseus conceals in the Cyclops' cave and later proudly—and, as it turns out, rashly—announces to his blinded enemy, that name by which later he proudly identifies himself at the court of the Phaeacians: "I am Odysseus, son of Laertes, known to all mankind for my crafty designs—my fame goes up to the heavens. . . ." *This* is the heroic self, the name which in the case of Odysseus, as in so many others, is a speaking name, with more than a hint in it of the hero's nature and destiny. But an individual personality is also suggested in those recurrent passages where a hero addresses some part of himself—his *thumos* or his *kradie,* his heart; the words used imply the central personality of the speaker, a personality to which the part addressed belongs. It might be added that Homer's reference to the diaphragm as the organ of the intelligence is no more surprising than our own frequent reference to the heart as the organ of the emotions or even of the intellect. Pascal knew all about the brain, but that didn't stop him from saying, "Le coeur a ses raisons," and a famous American senator once ran for higher office with the slogan "In your heart, you know he's right."

All this does not, of course, mean that Snell's careful analysis of Homer's language has to be rejected; his lexical approach has thrown light on many aspects of Homeric thought and feeling. What does not stand up to examination is his claim that the language reveals the absence of a conception of individual personality and that consequently discussion of character as a base for speech and action is, in the case of the Homeric poems, irrelevant and misleading.

Many scholars who repudiate the extreme position still feel it necessary to warn against the use of the word "character"; they give the impression that they think Snell is only half wrong. They claim that in Homer and, for that matter, in Greek tragedy, we do not find the fully developed personalities we are familiar with in modern literature. "However strong their impact as personalities"—I am quoting Albin Lesky, one of the most judicious scholars in this field—"they lack the wealth of individual features—often represented for their own sake—of their modern counterparts." He is obviously thinking of the novel—Emile Zola's gigantic creations, for example, or those of Thomas Mann; in *Buddenbrooks* the reader will find a plethora of "individual features . . . represented for their own sake." *For their own sake*—precisely! The fact that Homer does not carry this extra baggage is something to be thankful for; Shakespeare does not carry it either—he does not tell us what young Hamlet was studying at Wittenberg or how many children Lady Macbeth had. Homer's characters, like Shakespeare's, like those of all great art, are the product of creative genius working in a rich tradition and equipped with an exquisite sense of artistic economy and balance. This poet knew what so many of his successors never learned or else forgot, that, to quote Corinna's advice to Pindar, one should sow seeds with the hand, not the sack; Voltaire, many centuries later, put it another way: "The recipe for boredom is—completeness."

In any case, the proof of the pudding is in the eating. Homer's characters are in fact among the most individually striking and influential ever created. The later Greeks never tired of discussing, in prose and poetry, the nature of Achilles' pride, the suicidal wrath of Ajax, the versatility of Odysseus; they re-created these figures in terms of their own time on the tragic stage. And succeeding ages have followed their example; Bloom, Dedalus, and Molly are only the most recent of a long series of reembodiments of Homer's characters. Only Shakespeare can compete with Homer in this extraordinary power to impose his fictional personalities on the imagination of succeeding ages. Only scholars—and I speak of them with sympathy since I am one myself—could bring themselves to deny Homer the power to create literary character in the fullest sense of the words, in defiance of the brute fact that Homer's characters have fascinated and obsessed writers and readers for some twenty-five hundred years, longer than any other such set of personalities except the characters of the Hebrew Old Testament.

IV

The "inner man" is not the only area to be explored with new insights and technologies; attention has also been directed to two aspects of Greek and especially Athenian culture that the Victorians swept under the rug: slavery and the inferior position, one might even say subjection, of women. The Victorians were not alone in their indifference to the phenomenon of chattel and other kinds of slavery in Greece; as Sir Moses Finley acidly pointed out, the very full index to Werner Jaeger's three-volume work on the formation of the Athenian character, *Paideia,* first published in 1933, contained no entry for "slaves" or "slavery." Yet, Finley goes on to say, "there was no action, no belief or institution in Greco-Roman antiquity that was not, in one way or the other, affected by the possibility that someone involved might be a slave."

There were two things the Greek of the classical period prized above all others. One was *kleos,* fame: the admiration of his fellow men for his prowess as a soldier, an orator, or an athlete—particularly the last, for winners of events at Olympia and the other great games were so overwhelmed with honors and rewards that it was a commonplace in the odes poets wrote, on commission, to celebrate their victories, to remind them, in ways sometimes subtle and sometimes blunt, that they were not gods but mortals. The other thing they prized was *schole,* leisure: freedom from the drudgery of work, time to stroll in the columned porticos of the city and discuss politics, points of law, or the latest tragedy, to attend the law courts where suits were under judgment or the assembly where questions of policy, even of peace or war, were under discussion, to frequent the gymnasium, keep the body in shape, and at the same time admire the beauty of the young men who might well be listening to a snub-nosed, barefoot eccentric called Socrates. Slaves rarely make an appearance in the dialogues of Plato (an exception is the *Meno,* where a house-born slave boy is used for a demonstration that even the lowest form of human life has latent knowledge that can only have come from a previous existence), but without the slaves those long, leisurely conversations, in the gymnasia, the wrestling schools, the houses of the wealthy—Agathon, Callias, Polemarchus—and, exceptionally, by the banks of the Ilissus, could not have taken place. Finley is only one (Vidal-Naquet is another) of those historians who have investigated the "peculiar institution" of the Greeks in all its complexity and diversity—the chattel slaves, mostly of foreign origin, of Athens, the native Helots of Sparta and Penestae of Thessaly, the various forms of debt bondage, and the many other forms of dependence summarized in the ancient formula "between free and slave."

Slaves, however, were not the only prerequisite for those golden hours of leisure; someone had to run them. A man needed, in addition, a wife, whose excellence, according to one of Plato's characters, was to be demonstrated in her performance of "the duty of ordering the house well, looking after the property inside, and obeying her husband." What is meant by "ordering the house well" is made clear in another Socratic dialogue, this one by Xenophon, the *Oeconomicus*. It introduces us to a young gentleman, Ischomachus, who has just finished instructing his newlywed bride, a girl of less than fifteen years, in her duties; he tells Socrates, proudly, what he prescribed. She is to train and supervise a staff of domestic slaves, organize the efficient storage of equipment and supplies, store and manage the distribution of grain, wine, and oil, make and meet the annual budget, and see to the manufacture of household clothes from the raw fleece all the way to the finished garment. She is strongly urged not to use makeup of any kind and to avoid sitting by the fire; she is to be constantly on the move, checking, inspecting, helping. According to Ischomachus she accepted the program with enthusiasm. It is typical of the male Greek attitude that we are never told her name; she is just "the wife of Ischomachus." This faceless anonymity is in fact normal for respectable Athenian women; even in legal cases where their right or claim to property may be the issue they remain nameless. (One Athenian woman whose name does turn up in a courtroom speech, Neaera, is, according to the speaker, not an Athenian citizen and has had a remarkable career as a prostitute.) When Pericles, in the funeral speech, addressed a few cold words at the end of it to the widows of the men whose glorious death in battle he had just celebrated, telling them that *their* glory was to be least talked about, whether for good or evil, among men, he was only expressing the firm conviction of the average Athenian male.

Inside that house of which they were the managers and from which they rarely emerged, women must have been a formidable presence, and sometimes we get a glimpse of that aspect of the relations between the sexes, as in the *Lysistrata* of Aristophanes, where the play's heroine talks about wives asking husbands what they have been doing in the assembly today.

Too many times, as we sat in the house, we'd hear that
*   you'd done it*
again—manhandled another affair of state with your
*   usual*
staggering incompetence. Then, masking our worry
*   with a nervous laugh,*
we'd ask you, brightly, "How was the Assembly today,
*   dear? Anything*
in the minutes about Peace?" . . .

But since the books, inscriptions, and vase paintings on which we have to base our vision of Athenian home life were all made by men, who no doubt fully agreed with Pericles on the subject of women, such glimpses are rare.

Yet there was much more to be found and studied than previous generations had suspected (or wanted to find) and modern scholars, most of them women, have combed, reinterpreted, and assembled the evidence to re-create the life of ancient Greek and especially Athenian women from childhood through initiation rites of various kinds to marriage and motherhood in its legal, religious, and social context. Understandably, some of the female scholars who deal with this material strike a polemical note; one vigorous survey of the position of women in Athens at its political and artistic high point, the fifth century B.C.—a book remarkable for, among other things, its extraordinarily full coverage of the evidence from vase paintings—appeared under the title *The Reign of the Phallus*.

But there is one category of evidence that poses a problem—the picture of women that emerges not from the law court speeches, vases, and inscriptions but from poetry, the epic and the drama. For classical Greek literature presents us with an astonishing wealth of imposing female characters, in this respect far surpassing the Roman literature that was formed on the Greek model, and rivaling any literature of the medieval or modern world.

Homer's *Odyssey*, which in its present form is probably a product of the late eighth century B.C., gives us not only Penelope, the faithful and resourceful wife, but also Helen, the wife whose adultery caused a ten-year war and who now presides in queenly fashion over the court of the husband whom she abandoned; it gives us Nausicaa, one of the most charming—and intelligent—young women in all literature, as well as Circe, the enchantress who turns men into swine, and Calypso, the importunate divine mistress.

And Athenian tragedy, at the high point of the reign of the phallus, presents us with a succession of female characters who play leading roles, from Clytemnestra, the wronged and vengeful wife who towers over the male figures of the *Oresteia,* to Antigone, the young woman who, invoking divine law against human decrees, defies the power of the state; from Medea, the abandoned wife who makes her husband pay a terrible price for his ingratitude, to Electra, who, in Sophocles' play, never wavers from her resolve to avenge her father even when all hope seems lost; from Phaedra, wasting away from starvation as she tries, in vain, to resist the love for her stepson that Aphrodite has imposed on her, to Creusa and her passionate appeal to and denunciation of the god Apollo when she fears that he is not going to restore to her the child she secretly bore him. Only one of the surviving tragedies has no female character, and the titles and fragments of the hundreds of lost plays tell the same story: women, on the tragic stage, play the active roles, as man's partner or more often antagonist, that real life, according to our other sources, denied them.

One proposed explanation of this surprising situation is that all the characters, men and women alike, belong to a far-off mythical past and so have little or no relevance to the passions and concerns of the fifth-century audience. But this defies the realities of theatrical performance. Tragedy, Aristotle rightly says, should arouse pity and fear; it can do so only if it touches the deepest levels of its audience's hopes, wishes, and forebodings. And of course the Athenians did not think of the mythical heroes as far away and long ago; these figures were a forceful presence in the popular mind, ideal models or awful warnings. When Socrates, under indictment, refuses to save his life by abandoning what he considers his god-given mission, he cites the example of Achilles, who refused to save his life by abandoning his resolve to avenge his friend Patroclus. And when the sentence of death is handed down, he tells the court he looks forward to meeting, in the lower world, such heroes as Palamedes and Ajax, who, like him, were unjustly condemned. In any case, Shakespeare's theater too presents characters and places far off or long ago; not one of his plays is set in the late Elizabethan and early Jacobean context of his own time and country. And yet no one doubts that he lived up to Hamlet's prescription for the players and showed "the very age and body of the time his form and pressure."

It is true that with few exceptions, such as Aeschylus' Clytemnestra, Greek tragedy's women act purely in the domestic sphere, as virgins, wives, or mothers, or, if beyond it, like Electra, through men. Tragedy gives us a picture of a life on which our prose documents are silent, the inner life of the house, the intimacy of the relationships between husband and wife, mother and son, father and daughter. It is a picture of the wife and mother in that confined space where she is both queen and prisoner very different from that suggested by the bland eulogies of the funeral inscriptions. It suggests, what one would in fact have suspected, that in many cases the result of confining a wife to the house, the slaves, and the children was to create a potentially dangerous, explosive force.

Deep in their subconscious, in their dreams and nightmares, Greek men seem to have sensed this danger, for in their myths women appear repeatedly either as the willing sacrificial victim at the altar or as the killer, the murderer of the male. Women as the adversary came in the form of killers of male children like Medea and Procne, husband killers like Clytemnestra and Deianira, adulterous seducers turned killer when their advances were rejected, like Stheneboea and (in Euripides' first version) Phaedra. The myths even provided dangerous women in large groups, like the Amazons who fought against men on the battlefield, the fifty daughters of Danaus, forty-nine of whom slaughtered their husbands on their wedding night, or the women of the island of Lemnos who went to the extreme limit of defiance of the male hierarchy by murdering their husbands and marrying their slaves.

Tragedy eagerly embraced such themes. The chorus in Aeschylus' *Suppliants* are the daughters of Danaus; by threatening to hang themselves on the statues of the city's gods, they force a reluctant king into fighting a battle for them in which he loses his own life, and although the last two plays of the trilogy are lost we know that forty-nine of them duly murdered their husbands. In Sophocles' *Trachiniae,* Deianira (whose name means "husband killer") is the unwitting and unwilling agent of the death of her husband, Heracles. In the seventeen tragedies of Euripides that have survived intact, Phaedra, Electra, and Agave kill or help kill a man, Medea kills a man and her male children, Hecuba blinds a man, and Creusa tries to kill one, while on the other hand Alcestis gives her life to save her husband's, and Iphigenia, Macaria, and Polyxena are sacrificed at the altar by men. Women's voices are so insistent on the Euripidean stage that Aristophanes can have Euripides say, in the *Frogs,* that in his plays, "They all stepped up to speak their piece, the mistress spoke, the slave spoke too, / the master spoke, the daughter spoke, the grandma spoke."

Some feminist critics have developed the argument that such a concentration on women in the public performance of tragedy was simply a reinforcement of the dominant male ideology, a justification of the seclusion and repression of women. The plays, written by men and acted by an all-male cast, were performed at a public function of the male democracy; the decision to award first, second, and third prize was in the hands of male judges, and, even more important, the selection of the three playwrights who were to have their plays produced was also the prerogative of male officials. The plays, even those of Euripides, who has often been considered sympathetic to women, must have been a reaffirmation of the male values of Athenian society.

Interpretations along these lines have been advanced with greater or lesser degrees of subtlety, but even the most fair-minded and rewarding treatment of the role of women in tragedy, Froma Zeitlin's chapter called "Playing the Other" in *Nothing to Do with Dionysos?*, while it explores brilliantly the theme that "drama . . . tests masculine values only to find these alone inadequate to the complexities of the situation," also finds that "in the end tragedy arrives at closures that generally reassert male, often paternal, structures of authority."

It is true, of course, that women in tragedy, even in Euripides, are almost always agents of male destruction or willing sacrificial victims. But the trouble is that Euripides loads the dice against any easy acceptance of these situations at face value by his presentation of the male characters involved. Iphigenia gives her life for Greece, but the men for whom she gives it—Agamemnon, Menelaus, Calchas, Odysseus, even Achilles—are unmasked as the weaklings, braggarts, cowards, and base intriguers that they are. In the *Alcestis* a wife gives her own life to save her husband's in ideal Athenian wifely fashion, but the lines Euripides puts in her husband's mouth must have made the audience sit up. After all, if your wife agrees to die instead of you (and, incidentally, in the age of organ transplants this play could be less of a fairy tale than it was for the Athenians), you should know better than to react to her last dying wails with the customary formulas of the deathbed scene; you are the one husband in the world who cannot and must not say, as Admetus does, "In the name of the gods do not have the heart to abandon me—in the name of your children whom you will leave behind orphaned . . . raise your head up—be strong, endure—If you die I don't want to live." Above all, you don't say, "If I had the tongue and song of Orpheus, so that, enchanting Demeter's daughter or her husband by my music, I might have

taken you from Hades, I would have gone below and
neither Pluto's hound nor Charon the ferryman of souls
would have prevented me from bringing you back to life
and the light of the sun." After all, he didn't have to go
to such heroic lengths; he could just have died when his
time came. As if this were not enough to set one's teeth
on edge, Alcestis' death is followed by a quarrel between
the husband and his father, who, like his mother, de-
clined to take his place in the grave. It is the most electric
scene in the play, a sordid, bitter quarrel between two
blind egotists, staged over the body of the woman whose
self-sacrifice has made it possible for her husband to
denounce his mother and father as cowards and disown
them.

Jason, too, is condemned by his own words. Re-
minded by Medea that she saved his life in Colchis and
that to follow him she left behind not only her family
but also her status as a princess, he answers compla-
cently that he owes his success at Colchis not to Medea
but to Aphrodite alone of gods and men; Medea was so
madly in love with him that she couldn't help herself. In
any case, he goes on to say, she has been amply repaid
for what little she did do for him. "You left a savage
country, to live in Greece; here you have known justice.
. . ." Medea will kill her two sons and Jason will lose not
only them but his bride and her father and his hope of a

new kingdom, but after this speech it is hard to feel anything for him but contempt. And the end of the play is no reassertion of "male . . . structures of authority." Jason is abandoned even by the gods he appeals to; they send down a magic chariot in which Medea escapes from Corinth. What is more, it is in this play that one of the fundamental male structures of authority is specifically repudiated—the ideal of martial glory, the sanctification of male heroic death in battle that is so memorable a feature of Pericles' funeral speech. *"They* say," Medea tells the chorus of Corinthian women, *"they* say we live a life free from danger in the house, while they fight, spear in hand. What fools! I'd be ready to take my stand in the shield line three times rather than give birth just once." That biological function that was for the Greek male chauvinist the only justification for woman's existence—"There ought to have been some other way," says Jason later on in the play, "for men to breed sons . . ."—that despised but necessary function is here given pride of place above the martial valor that was the highest virtue of the man and citizen.

∎ ∎ ∎

V

The relocation of Attic tragedy in its social and religious context has added much to our understanding of it, but the attempt to cut it down to size, to make it a prisoner of its environment, limited in scope by the constraints of Athenian male ideology, is a waste of effort. The genie cannot be put back in the bottle. For great literature, though fashioned for and by its time and place, always reaches out beyond, speaking to later generations as well; it is, to use the terms of Jonson's eulogy of Shakespeare, not only of an age but for all time. Many of the greatest poets in fact are more fully appreciated by later ages than by their own; they foreshadow and help create the sensibilities of the generations to come. Euripides is a case in point; in the centuries that followed the end of Athens' great age, Aeschylus and Sophocles were revered as classics, but Euripides was performed. We have a vivid reminder of this fact in the shape of a broken piece of stone, part of an inscription of the fourth century B.C. recording the names of the nine tragedies offered by three poets at the Great Dionysia, together with the name of the author of the "old tragedy" regularly offered at this time in addition to the new ones. It covers the years 341, 340, and 339 B.C., and in each year the "old tragedy" was by Euripides.

And, of course, he is not the only one to survive on the later stage. In recent years the plays of all three Greek tragic masters, in translation and adaptation, have found fresh audiences on stage and screen; in theaters from Berlin to Edinburgh, from New York to San Diego, they speak to us as if the centuries between our time and theirs had never been. In theaters all over the world versions of Sophocles' *Antigone,* prominent among them those of Anouilh and Brecht, have faced modern audiences with the problem Sophocles posed to his Athenian audience—the clash of loyalties, to the state and to older, higher obligations. In Ireland, at Derry, the Irish poet Seamus Heaney recently produced his version of the *Philoctetes* of Sophocles, a play about a victim of injustice so embittered by suffering and by brooding on his wrongs that when salvation and a cure for his debilitating disease is offered by his enemies, for their own cynical purposes, he cannot bring himself to accept it; it takes a voice from the heavens to change his mind. Heaney wrote into what is for the most part a faithful as well as brilliant version of the Sophoclean play a moral for his country and his times:

> *History says,* Don't hope
> On this side of the grave.

But then, once in a lifetime
The longed-for tidal wave
Of justice can rise up,
And hope and history rhyme.

So hope for a great sea-change
On the far side of revenge.
Believe that a further shore
Is reachable from here.
Believe in miracles
And cures and healing wells.

And we have seen, too, *Iphigenia in Aulis* played in New York as a protest against our war in Vietnam, and a French version of Euripides' *Trojan Women* produced in Paris as a protest against the French war in Algeria.

The Greeks are still very much with us. Even that strange ritual of sacrifice with which we started, which seemed the epitome of "otherness," so alien to our thought and feeling, has its resonances in our world. We, too, might need some equivalent of the "comedy of innocence" if we had to kill a domestic animal with our own hands every time we ate meat. As it is, we leave the business of killing to others, and try not to think about it. But in recent years many of us have indeed begun to think about it, to face the mechanical horrors of the stockyard slaughterhouse and, still worse, the refined cruelty of a system that raises animals confined and force-fed in narrow cages, so that even before its death the victim is deprived of any real life. Some of us have turned away altogether from eating meat, enough of us so that public institutions and airlines make provisions for vegetarian meals. And in the ancient world, too, there were those—Pythagoreans and Orphics—who refused to take part in the sacrifice and the consumption of meat, even though it cut them off from the community and made them a people apart, and sometimes persecuted.

In fact, when one thinks again of that list of things that Louis MacNeice, an Anglo-Irishman writing in Hampstead in 1938, found so unimaginably different, one cannot help feeling that to us they seem all too familiar. "When I should remember the paragons of Hellas," he wrote,

I think instead
Of the crooks, the adventurers, the opportunists,
   The careless athletes and the fancy boys,
The hair-splitters, the pedants, the hard-boiled sceptics
   And the Agora and the noise

Of the demagogues and the quacks; and the women
    pouring
Libations over graves
And the trimmers at Delphi and the dummies at Sparta
    and lastly
I think of the slaves.

The agora is the marketplace, for which we have sub-
stituted the shopping mall. Women today don't pour
libations on graves, but we have our macabre funeral
parlors, where the late lamented, embalmed and
touched up for the occasion, makes a last appearance for
relatives and friends. Our trimmers are not at Delphi;
they are much closer to home. And our dummies are not
at Sparta; but we have them—in spades. As for the
slaves, Americans need no reminder that one hundred
and fifty years ago there were slaves and slave owners on
both sides of the Potomac.

In fact, when we think of the two great flaws in
Athenian democracy that recent scholarship has explored and emphasized, we ought to remember not only
that slavery and male dominance were characteristic of
all ancient societies but also that we, of all people, have
no right to cast the first stone. Pericles' proud claim for
Athenian democracy—power in the hands of the people,

equality before the law—does not mention the slaves, but our Declaration of Independence—"that all men are created equal"—does not mention them either, although the man who drafted it and many of those who signed it were owners of African slaves. That wrong was finally righted only by a bloody and destructive civil war, but we are still suffering the consequences of those many years of injustice; the wound in the commonweal is not healed yet, and we have to pray and believe, like Heaney, that "a further shore / Is reachable from here," that "hope and history" may "rhyme."

As for the other flaw, the exclusion of women from Athenian public life, we should not forget that women in these United States had to struggle for more than half a century before the Nineteenth Amendment to the Constitution gave them full voting rights in 1920; that Great Britain reluctantly made the same concession in 1928; and that the French took the last word of the revolutionary slogan *liberté, égalité, fraternité* so literally that French women were not given the right to vote until 1945.

This does not entitle us, of course, to discard the results of the reevaluation of Greek culture that has emphasized its "otherness," the attitudes and institutions that resemble those of Egypt and Babylon, not to mention those of Lafitau's Algonquins, Hurons, and Iroquois. But we should not forget the astonishing originality that sets them apart, that makes them unique. They invented democracy more than two thousand years before any modern Western nation took the first steps toward it; they invented not only philosophy and the theater but also the model of a national literature, with its canon of great writers, its critics and commentators, its libraries; they invented organized competitive athletics—it is not for nothing that the recent sports that took place at Barcelona were called Olympics; they invented political theory, rhetoric, biology, zoology, the atomic theory—one could go on. Above all, in startling contrast to the magnificent but static civilizations of the great Eastern river valleys—Tigris, Euphrates, and Nile—they created in the restless turbulence of their tiny city-states that impatient rhythm of competition and innovation that has been the distinguishing characteristic of Western civilization ever since. Though we can no longer say, with Shelley, that we are all Greeks, nor claim, as the Victorians might have claimed, that GREEKS "я" US, we must always acknowledge how greatly, how deeply, how irrevocably, we are in their debt.

Two

THE WALLS OF THEBES

I

The word "humanities" is, to describe it charitably, a rather loose term, a holdall for a group of disciplines which are clearly distinguishable, in method as in field of study, from the sciences, but hard to define as an entity. Does it include, for example, the self-styled social sciences? If history is a social science, obviously yes; anthropology, certainly; sociology, maybe (it depends on who is writing it); political science, perhaps, on the grounds that since it is obviously not a science it must belong to the humanities; and possibly economics, which, to judge by recent predictions and assessments made by its practitioners, is a form of metaphysical speculation. Do the humanities include the arts? The history of art, obviously, but what about the practice of the arts—of painting, sculpture, music, drama, dance? This is one point on which a ruling has been made by no less an authority than the federal government: it has set up a National Endowment for the Arts as well as a National Endowment for the Humanities. There is, however, one common feature which can serve to distinguish the humanities from science on the one hand and performance on the other: the fact that their typical medium of expression is the written word. The case is well put in a passage of the recent *Report of the Commission on the Humanities:* "Rooted in language and dependent in particular on writing, the humanities are inescapably bound to literacy." And one might add, not just to literacy, but to literature. The *Shorter Oxford Dictionary* defines them as "learning or literature concerned with human culture; a term including the various branches of polite scholarship, as grammar, rhetoric, poetry, and especially the study of the ancient Latin and Greek classics."

The principal objects of humane study, its texts, not only Dante, Goethe, Homer, Molière, Shakespeare, and Virgil but also the classics of history, of moral and political philosophy—Gibbon, Macaulay, Machiavelli, Nietzsche, Plato, Rousseau—are works of literature. A further common characteristic of the humanities is their emphasis on the past. We do not by any means neglect the present but realize that our main emphasis must fall on the great traditions of art, thought, and literature which have formed the minds and hearts of our predecessors and which, interpreted afresh in each generation, can bring us new understanding of ourselves and the world we live in.

These studies—I hardly need to say it here—are now facing grim prospects. Their principal area of activity, the old liberal or general education system, is today, in the words of a Carnegie Foundation Report, "a disaster area," and the latest generation of students, facing a shrinking and more demanding job market, are inclined to dismiss the humanities as a luxury and choose programs which make the attractive offer (though it often turns out to be illusory) that they will prepare students specifically and directly for the professions and the world of business.

The students' attitude is understandable; the humanities, unlike so many other subjects offered by the university, seem to be a field studied for itself alone. The sciences offer an entrée to the lucrative worlds of industrial and military research, medicine, and engineering; for those who aim at business or law, courses with obvious contemporary reference seem more attractive than what the humanities can provide. What will the study of Baudelaire, Chaucer, Ovid, Schiller, Sophocles, and Spinoza, of quattrocento painting or baroque music equip you for? To be a teacher of the humanities seems the only obvious answer, and the prospects of gainful employment and advancement in that field today are far from inviting.

There was a time, of course, when the study of the humanities, in particular its core subjects, Latin and Greek, was indeed the key to success in the outside world. All through the nineteenth century the British Empire was run, and on the whole run rather well, by civil servants who had read Greats at Oxford or for the Tripos at Cambridge, had become Platonists or Aristotelians, and had learned to compose flawless Greek iambic and Latin elegiac verse. There was a lot to be said for the advice given to the young by Thomas Gaisford in his Christmas sermon at Christ Church, Oxford, sometime in the middle of the century: "Nor can I do better, in conclusion, than impress upon you the study of Greek literature, which not only elevates above the vulgar herd but leads not infrequently to positions of considerable emolument." But the world has changed. The British army no longer demands competence in Latin from candidates for its military academy, as it did in the days of Stalky and Co., and, if I may judge from what I see of the ruling circles of this country in Washington, the aspirant to high administrative employment should, if he happens to be well acquainted with literature, especially foreign literature, conceal that guilty secret until he attains a position of relative security. A love for and knowledge of literature and the arts is of little practical advantage in the modern world and may even, by raising suspicion that its owner considers himself, in Gaisford's phrase, "elevated above the vulgar herd," turn out to be an actual disadvantage.

The fact that Gaisford felt the need to "impress" on his audience the study of Greek literature reveals the existence of a dissident view, and it was indeed not long before the scientists unmasked their batteries: Huxley, for example, pronounced in 1880 a funeral oration for literary studies—*belles lettres,* he called them—at the opening of Josiah Mason's Science College (no classics taught) in Birmingham, a real-life equivalent of Dickens's Coketown, where Mr. Gradgrind's staff taught scientific and practical subjects rather than the classics. But though Gaisford, in the great tradition of the eccentric Oxford don, was stating the case for the most obviously impractical element of the humanities in the most extreme and outrageous terms, his two basic assertions, that this type of study admitted its adepts to the elite club of the cultured and also led to worldly advancement, continued long after his day to be the main arguments (though not so crudely expressed) for humane studies. Both of them were still current as late as 1938, when Louis MacNeice wrote, cynically and frankly, about his Oxford career in *litterae humaniores* which had won him, not indeed considerable emolument, but a fairly well-paid job as a professor of Greek (in, of all places, Birmingham):

> *. . . the so-called humane studies*
>   *May lead to cushy jobs*
> *But leave the men who land them spiritually bankrupt*
>   *Intellectual snobs.*
> *Not but what I am glad to have my comforts,*
>   *Better authentic mammon than a bogus god;*
> *If it were not for Lit. Hum., I might be climbing*
>   *A ladder with a hod.*

The claim that these studies elevated "above the common herd" was championed, not long after Gaisford's sermon, by no less an authority than Matthew Arnold, who proclaimed the necessity, for the fully formed human being, of "culture," which he defined as "the acquainting ourselves with the best that has been known and said in the world and thus with the history of the human spirit." It was his hope that such culture would replace that religious faith which, once a full sea, was now an ebb tide, its sound a "melancholy, long, withdrawing roar." Since at the same time he divided the population of Great Britain into barbarians (the aristocracy), philistines (the middle classes), and something he called simply "Populace," he can hardly have envisaged this new religion as a mass phenomenon; Oxford men might possibly find in Homer the emotional stimulus they no longer received from the sacraments and music of the Church of England, but the working man was not likely to accept Plato as a substitute for the Methodist chapel. What Arnold was calling for, in fact, was an intellectual elite based on humane studies, an idea which reappears in burlesque form as MacNeice wryly recalls his Oxford training in philosophy:

> . . . *certainly it was fun while it lasted*
> *And I got my honours degree*
> *And was stamped as a person of intelligence and*
>   *culture*
> *For ever wherever two or three*
> *Persons of intelligence and culture*
>   *Are gathered together in talk*

Writing definitions on invisible blackboards
In non-existent chalk.

Both these defenses of the liberal education were in effect claims that it prepared its devotees for and indeed provided them with what the Greeks called the good life *(to eu zen)*—living well. It paved the way to employment which guaranteed material prosperity and at the same time equipped its graduates for intellectual and aesthetic appreciation of "the best which has been thought and said in the world." But there was one more claim made in defense of these studies: that they prepared the young for "the good life" in another sense, Socrates' sense, the life of moral excellence; that they produced, in fact, the good citizen. This argument appeared in classic form on the lips of yet another Oxford don: his name was Copleston, and after emphasizing the practical value of classical studies (practical in the Gaisford sense), he added that they also "communicate to the mind . . . a high sense of honour, a disdain of death in a good cause, a passionate devotion to the welfare of one's country." This claim, too, is given rough handling by MacNeice:

But the classical student is bred to the purple, his
training in syntax

Is also a training in thought
And even in morals; if called to the bar or the barracks
He always will do what he ought.

If the case for the humanities cannot do more than ring the changes on these three shopworn (if not actually spurious) arguments—that they are the royal road to riches, the ticket of admission to the elite intellectual club, and the path to patriotic glory and the grave—there would be little point in advocating their study.

In the end MacNeice can see only one positive result (besides his relatively cushy job) of his studies in the liberal arts:

. . . in case you should think my education was wasted
    I hasten to explain
That having once been to the University of Oxford
    You can never really again
Believe anything that anyone says and that of course is
        an asset
    In a world like ours . . . .

A melancholy conclusion, to say the least. And the present student generation has no need to learn disbelief; what it needs is something to believe.

It is one of the distinguishing characteristics of humane studies, as I observed before, that they turn to the past to gain perspective on the present. And if we look back at the long history of liberal education and humane studies, and particularly to their earliest manifestations and origins, we can take a certain comfort from the realization that we are not the first who have had to make a case for them to a skeptical and, to use Arnold's term, philistine audience.

II

The modern disillusion with the humanities begins in the nineteenth century; it stems from the sudden, simultaneous expansion of industry, the physical sciences, and engineering, together with large-scale industrial employment and the first steps toward universal education at fairly high levels. For many centuries before the nineteenth, higher education had been the privileged enclosure of a small ruling class, its function to prepare men for the church, the law, and politics, in a society which thought in terms of stability rather than progress and in which the changes that were eventually to produce the Industrial Revolution were a slow process of maturation rather than a series of upheavals. Over the whole medieval and early modern period, in spite of constant readjustment, modifications, additions, and widening of scope, the higher education of the West retained the basic form and essence of the old set of *artes liberales* which the early Middle Ages had inherited from the Romans. That word *liberales* connects the *quadrivium* and *trivium* of the Middle Ages and late antiquity with republican Rome of the first and second centuries B.C. It precisely characterizes what Cicero, for example, regarded as the proper study of a Roman: things proper for a free man, *liber,* as opposed to a slave (whose skills, if any, were merely technical), proper also for a *liberalis,* a man of noble, aristocratic outlook and action. These attitudes had been taken over from the Greeks, who regarded leisure, *schole,* as the indispensable condition of the good life and the characteristic condition of free men; "slaves," so ran a Greek proverb, "have no leisure"—it was a definition.

The Romans, an immensely practical people, had welded Italy into a solid imperial base from which they won control of Sicily, most of Spain, North Africa, and Greece before they came into contact with and developed the need for the kind of literary culture on which the Greeks of the Hellenistic period prided themselves. Prior to that contact with the Greek East, the Roman ideal of manhood included no slot for literary or humane studies. The funeral eulogy of a Roman aristocrat pronounced in the year 221 B.C. ran as follows: "he had attained the ten supreme goods that wise men spend their lives in search of: he had been a great soldier, a fine orator, a courageous commander; he had been responsible for great enterprises, he had been first magistrate; he possessed the highest wisdom, he had been first among the members of the senate, he had acquired a great fortune by honest means, he had left many children behind him and he had been famous in the Republic." Two of those "supreme goods"—"highest wisdom" and "fine orator"—sound as if they may have some connection with intellectual culture, but the "wisdom" was almost certainly practical, and at the time in question Roman oratory, not yet influenced by Greek theory and practice, was a matter of plain, businesslike speaking with no claim to literary merit.

Horace gives us a vivid picture of Roman life before it was transformed by contact with the Greeks. "For ages at Rome it was a pleasure and a duty to get up at dawn and open the house to visitors, to lay down the law to dependents, dispense funds, under bond, to reliable borrowers, to take advice from the old and to tell the young how to increase their assets by putting a brake on ruinous indulgence." But after "captured Greece had taken

its fierce conqueror captive and brought the arts to rustic
Latium," the Roman "applied his wits to Greek literature and . . . began to inquire what useful contribution
could be made by Sophocles, Thespis and Aeschylus."
The Roman aristocracy learned Greek, studied Greek
literature in Latin translation (the first literary work in
Latin was a translation of Homer's *Odyssey* made by a
Greek prisoner of war), and began to create a literature
of its own, based on Greek models for the most part, yet
recognizably different in tone and emphasis, a Roman,
not a Greek, voice.

There were protests, of course. Cato the Elder, for example, "had an aversion to philosophy"—so Plutarch
tells us—"and heaped abuse on all Greek culture and
education." He ridiculed the school of Isocrates, saying
that his pupils went on studying until they were old men,
as if they were getting ready to use their rhetorical technique pleading their case before Minos in Hades. And he
prophesied that when the Romans had become incura-
bly infected by Greek literature, they would lose their
empire. He cannot have been alone in this distrust of the
new studies, for even Cicero, who spoke fluent Greek
and peppered his letters with Greek phrases, who translated, adapted, and plagiarized the work of Greek phi-

losophers (and in doing so gave western Europe its philosophical vocabulary), even Cicero, when he is speaking in public, before a court or the Senate, is apt to assume an air of ignorant indifference to Greek cultural phenomena, just to show that he is not completely infected—that he is still in some respects an old-fashioned Roman. In his prosecution of the provincial governor of Sicily, who had appropriated Greek works of art by the cartload, Cicero mentions two bronze statues of girls carrying baskets on their head and affects ignorance of a Greek name: "The statues themselves are called the Basket-carriers and the artist—what is his name? Who *was* it?—Yes, thank you sir, quite right—it was Polyclitus."

Cicero himself, out of the courtroom and writing books on oratory and philosophy, takes humanistic studies for granted (though he is capable of claiming that the learning—*doctrina*—the Romans took over from the Greeks was improved in the process). But there is one famous occasion on which he came out roundly in defense of these studies in court—in his plea for the Greek poet Archias, whose Roman citizenship had been questioned by some political enemies of his patron Lucullus. Cicero deals with the facts and the legal aspects of the case in short order; his main line of defense is, as he says, "novel and unconventional." He asks the court's permission, given the nature of the defendant's profession, to dilate a little on "literature and the liberal arts" *(de studiis humanitatis ac litterarum)*. He proposes to convince the court that his client's profession and achievement are such that if he were not actually a Roman citizen (as Cicero will prove he is) he ought to be made one on the spot.

The case for poetry, in a Roman court, has to rest partly at least on its usefulness—*utile* is the word Horace uses to describe what the Romans thought tragedy might bring them. And Cicero uses what we might call the Copleston defense—that literature instills a "high sense of honor . . . a passionate devotion to the welfare of one's country," produces, in fact, the good citizen. Since the speaker happens to be Marcus Tullius Cicero, he unblushingly uses himself as an example: it was the inspiration drawn from wide reading which enabled him to save Rome at risk of his own life from Catiline and his fellow conspirators. "All literature, all philosophical treatises, all the voices of antiquity," he says, "are full of examples for imitation, which would all lie unseen in darkness without the light of literature." Cicero is addressing a jury made up of hardheaded Roman men of property—those whose portrait busts enrich our museums with faces that would be perfectly at home in a group photograph of the board of General Motors—and as if he suddenly realized that some of his audience might be offended by the implication that anyone *not* addicted to reading might be incapable of great actions, he hastens to hedge his bet: "Some men have attained greatness without the help of culture, simply through a natural, almost heaven-sent disposition." The point he wishes to emphasize, however, is that the combination of such a disposition with liberal culture produces something uniquely noble and brilliant.

From this exquisite modulation of the Copleston defense he proceeds to a Ciceronian version of the Arnold. Even if these studies have no such useful results and provide only delight, "you would have to agree," he tells his hearers, "that there is no mental exercise more civilized and proper for a free citizen" *(humanissimam ac liberalissimam)*. "Other activities," he goes on in words which have justly become famous, "are subject to limitation by the facts of season, age or place; but these studies sustain us in youth and delight us in old age; they add to our joy in prosperity, they provide refuge and comfort in adversity; they give pleasure at home and advancement abroad; they pass the night hours with us, accompany us on the road, share our holidays in the country." I need make no apology on this occasion for repeating his words in the language in which he wrote them:

haec studia adolescentiam alunt, senectutem
oblectant, secundas res ornant, adversis
perfugium ac solacium praebent, delectant
domi, non impediunt foris, pernoctant
nobiscum, peregrinantur, rusticantur.

Cicero began the speech by explaining his particular interest in the case; he attributes whatever skill he may
have as an orator (and whatever public service that skill
may have furnished the Republic) to the instruction and
advice given him by his client, the Greek poet whose
citizenship is in question. He realizes that some members of the court may be surprised by this statement;
Archias is a poet and one who writes in Greek at that.
What connection can there be between Greek poetry
and the practical ability, indispensable for political and
social advancement in the Roman world, to speak con-
vincingly in public? Cicero's answer is worth remember-
ing. He has never, he says, devoted himself exclusively
to one professional study—rhetoric, the law. "For all
the liberal arts, those which are concerned with humanity, are linked by an imperceptible bond of common
relationship." He realizes that this plea for poetry as an
essential element in the education of a public speaker
and statesman would come as a surprise to his Roman

audience; it is one of the reasons why he asks their indulgence for his "novel and unconventional line of defense." But it would not have sounded at all strange to
the Greeks from whom the Romans had inherited the
program and even the conception of a liberal education.
For when the studies we call the humanities made their
first appearance, in the Athens of the fifth century B.C.,
they did so as a program of adult education which was
designed to produce accomplished, persuasive public
speakers, and, though rhetorical competence was clearly
the principal objective, the program included, in rudi-
mentary form, all our liberal arts and laid especially
heavy stress on the interpretation of poetry. Rhetoric
was not an isolated discipline; it was in fact, as scholars
of the early Middle Ages proudly claimed, the queen and
mother of the liberal arts.

III

Rhetoric and its ancillary disciplines owed their birth in
the second half of the fifth century B.C. to something that
had happened over half a century before: the establishment in Athens of a form of government called *demo-*

kratia—literally translated, the people in power—which made the assembly of free citizens the sovereign authority in the state. It was at first a very conservative democracy, its mainstay the farmers of Attica who owned armor and formed the battle line which defeated a Persian force at Marathon in 490 B.C., to the astonishment of both sides. When the Persians came back in force they burned Athens to the ground but the Athenians had taken to the sea; their fleet played a key role in the defeat of the Persian navy at Salamis, the decisive battle of the war. Athens then used its fleet to liberate the Greek cities of the Aegean islands and the Asian Minor coasts; it proceeded to organize them in a league which became a naval empire. And these achievements changed the nature of democracy: the revenues of empire, the safety of the state depended now not on the farmers who formed the infantry line but on the urban poor who manned the war galleys. By mid-century the new power relationships were beginning to find political form, and curbs on full popular sovereignty were weakened or removed; the great age of Periclean imperial democracy started on its splendid, short-lived career. This new way of life and government created the need for a new education, or rather, in the sense that education is a preparation to play an active, even leading, role in a community of equals, something that had never existed before. The decision by majority vote, sovereign in every aspect of daily life from assembly decisions on peace or war to the most insignificant lawsuits brought before a jury, made the art of persuasion not only the key to success in public life but also an essential weapon of self-defense in private and business affairs.

Of course, there had been persuasive speakers long before democracy was thought of; Odysseus is the mythical prototype of the great orator. But such skill was a gift of the gods: either you had it or you didn't. And in a closed aristocratic society you would not have too much need for it; aristocratic minds tend to think alike. The young aristocrat did not need eloquence to win a place in society; it was already won. All he had to do was to measure up to the standards of his fathers: to be preeminent in battle, to bring glory on his family at the great athletic games, to play the lyre and sing the traditional songs at the symposium. But none of this was thought of as education; the aristocrat knows by instinct—by blood, he would say—the duties and privileges of his caste. It is characteristic of an aristocracy in fact to find education rather suspect; a man who has to learn the way things are done is by definition an outsider. "The wise man is he who knows much by nature, just by being what he is," said Pindar, singing the praises of the aristocratic virtues in the century which saw them go under.

As for learning, "a man can learn and yet see darkly
. . . walking always on uncertain feet, his mind unfinished and fed with scraps of a thousand virtues." This
sorry makeshift is contrasted with the aristocratic hero
par excellence, Achilles, trained by the centaur Chiron
to hunt lions: "the splendor running in the blood has
much weight."

But these words were the swan song of a dying ideal;
Athenian democracy had changed the world forever. It
is true that the old families still dominated Athenian
politics, but they did not do so by god-given authority;
the "splendor running in the blood" had to learn some
new tricks. The statesman now had to be elected; to
influence policy he had to persuade the assembly, and at
the end of his term of office he had to account for his
actions before his fellow citizens. Even if he renounced
political power, he still needed the persuasive arts, for in
the new Athenian law courts, as in the assembly, a man
spoke for himself, not through a lawyer. And in Athens
the courts, safeguard of the new democracy, sat in con-
tinuous session; the Athenians then (as now) were a liti-
gious lot, very apt to go to law about anything at all.
There can have been few Athenians who did not sooner
or later appear in court as prosecutor or in self-defense.
And here again, though birth and wealth did no harm,
persuasion was essential. "To the eye of persuasion I

give all praise," said the goddess Athena in the tragedy of Aeschylus which commemorated the foundation of Athens' oldest court of law. Persuasion was the oil which made the wheels of Athenian democracy go round.

Of course, there were men in real life who, like Odysseus in myth, had a natural talent for persuasive speaking. Themistocles was such a man; the caliber of his eloquence can be judged from the fact that he persuaded the Athenians to use the wealth accruing from the discovery of new veins of silver on the construction of a fleet rather than distributing the proceeds at so much per head. But there were few such born orators, and in a political climate which placed so high a value on the capacity to speak persuasively there would inevitably develop a demand for men who could teach the art. It was soon met. The teachers were the men, most of them foreigners, not Athenians, who are generally known as the Sophists.

Until Plato in the next century made this word a term of abuse, it was the normal Greek word to describe an expert—a poet, a musician, a craftsman, anyone who was master of a professional skill. And the Sophists— Protagoras, Gorgias, Hippias, and many another famous name—were, first and foremost, professionals in the art of persuasion. Protagoras offered to teach, for a price (and a very high one incidentally), how to make the weaker case appear the stronger. This, of course, is the essence of the art of persuasion; it is the man with the weaker case who needs the rhetoric. But Protagoras, like the others, was more than a teacher of rhetoric, for it was not enough to teach a man debating techniques; in an expanding and inquisitive society he needed not only methods of expression but something to express. He needed an acquaintance with literature, with what we call political science, with anthropology, psychology, history, with all those subjects which now constitute our so-called liberal education.

We have only a few fragments of the books the Sophists wrote; later generations let them vanish, while sedulously recopying every word Plato, the Sophists' great adversary, ever wrote (and a great many he didn't). But from the fragments, from some other scattered sources, and above all from the brilliant, if slanted, dramatic re-creations of the Sophists at work contained in the Platonic dialogues we can with some confidence reconstruct the nature and range of their educational program. Rhetoric, the technique of public speaking, was of course the core, the part for which the clients paid substantial amounts of hard cash. Protagoras announced that for every statement there was a counterstatement, and he trained his students in the technique of *antilogia*—speech and counterspeech. The student speaks on both sides of the question, displaying his greatest ingenuity on the weaker side; Protagoras claimed to teach how to make the weaker cause appear the stronger (the Greek words could also suggest that he could make the worse cause appear the better). The Greeks were in any case a people inclined to express themselves in antitheses, and they took enthusiastically to this system of argumentation. The evidence is to be seen everywhere in fifth-century literature—in the balanced pairs of speeches in Thucydides, the specimen legal speeches of Antiphon, the formal debates characteristic of Euripidean tragedy. In most instances the case is so highly developed on both sides that it is difficult to decide for one or the other, especially in the Thucydidean paired arguments for and against a particular policy. It is no accident that Protagoras is the author of the first succinct and memorable formulation of relativism, that the individual is the measure of all things, of the existence of the existent and the nonexistence of the nonexistent.

A rhetorical technique implied and instilled a philosophical viewpoint. It was not the only one. The argument from probability, designed for defense in cases for which no favorable evidence could be adduced and hostile witnesses had to be countered—"is it probable that I would assault a man taller or stronger than myself?"—produced a frame of mind which invoked the criterion of probability in wider fields. We see it at work in Thucydides' brilliant reconstruction of early Greek history as well as in the frequent critiques of prophecy and, for that matter, divine myth which we meet in Euripidean tragedy. A rhetorical tactic designed specifically for the political assembly, an appeal to expediency, was an argument shaped to counter invocations of justice, tradition, the sanctity of oaths or treaties by playing on the shortsighted idea of its own interests held by the mass of the audience. It was the base of the highly developed intellectual theories of realpolitik which we encounter in the Thucydidean speeches, those speeches which Hobbes so admired and which have remained classic statements of such doctrine ever since. One last rhetorical defense, an appeal to nature as against convention, custom, and law, gave a renewed impetus to an old controversy and also gave rise to the idea of the superman, who refuses to be bound by convention, whom we see described by Callicles in Plato's dialogue the *Gorgias*.

But rhetorical training, with its philosophical and critical spin-off, was not the whole of the Sophists' program; they also discoursed and wrote on subjects which clearly identify them as the first professors of the humanities. For one thing, they all claimed to be interpreters of poetry and to teach that skill to their pupils: "My opinion," says Plato's Protagoras, "is that the most important part of a man's education is the ability to discuss poetry intelligently." The Greeks had no sacred ethical or religious text, no Bible; the authorities to which they customarily appealed on questions of conduct and belief were the poets, especially Hesiod and Homer. So that a discussion of poetry, though it might begin, as it does in Protagoras' case, as a literary critique, moved easily and imperceptibly into the moral and political spheres, as it does in this instance; Protagoras continues to pursue the question at issue, the teachability of virtue, but "transferred," as he puts it, "to poetry," in this case a lyric poem of Simonides. There is evidently nothing unusual about this, for the method is accepted by the other Sophists, Prodicus and Hippias, as well as by the opponent, Socrates, who proceeds in fact to end this part of the discussion with some brazenly overingenious hermeneutics which are clearly Plato's satirical dismissal of such an approach to ethical questions.

Protagoras was noted, too, for his own original writings. He was the author of a famous book called *On the Primitive State of Man,* a history of human progress; its contents and spirit are almost certainly reflected in the

great ode of Sophocles' *Antigone* and underlie the myth
of the origin of justice put in his mouth by Plato in the
dialogue which bears his name. He also wrote a book,
On the Gods, which, to judge by the first sentence (all
we have) maintained an agnostic stance. He seems to
have developed a theory that the purpose of punishing
criminals should be not revenge but their rehabilitation,
and we are also told that he drew up the laws for the
new pan-Hellenic colony founded at Thurii, in Italy,
under Athenian leadership. The other great Sophists
were just as versatile. Prodicus was famous for his at-
tempts to rationalize religious myth and also for his
careful distinction between apparent synonyms, which
makes him the archetype of linguists and analytical philosophers. (His method is the target of an exquisite satire in Plato's dialogue.) Even Gorgias, who claimed to
teach nothing but the art of persuasion and cast scorn on
those, particularly Protagoras, who made wider claims,
provided a philosophical base for the amoral neutrality
of his rhetoric with a famous philosophical statement of
the impossibility of true knowledge. As for Hippias, he
was so versatile that, in addition to offering the usual
rhetorical training, he taught, among other things, as-
tronomy, geometry, arithmetic, grammar, mythology,
and history, including the history of philosophy and
mathematics. In Plato's dialogue, Protagoras dismisses

such studies as too technical; for himself he makes the extraordinary claim that his teaching will confer on his pupils sounder judgment in both private and public business, enable them to manage their family affairs in the best possible manner, and exert paramount influence both by speech and by action in the life of the community. "You mean," says Socrates, "that you teach the art of politics and promise to make men good citizens?" And Protagoras answers, "That is an exact definition of what I profess to offer."

It is often said that the importance of Socrates in the history of Western thought is that he brought theory down from the skies, from cosmological speculation, to the human world, to the moral and political problems of mankind. But this was in fact the achievement of the Sophists, who created an education designed for the first great democracy. Of course, their teaching and still more the new, often skeptical attitudes it generated contributed to the intellectual revolution which in the last quarter of the fifth century B.C. undermined age-old religious and moral beliefs, as well as traditional political loyalties. But it is an exaggeration to place on the shoulders of the Sophists full responsibility for the breakdown of traditional morality and religion in the late fifth

century. Thucydides attributes the loss of faith and religion not to the teaching of the Sophists but to the horrors of the plague of 430–427 B.C. And though the
speeches he puts in the mouths of Cleon and Alcibiades
owe their form to Sophistic rhetoric, there is no reason
to think that if there had been no Sophists at all the male
population of Scione and Melos would have escaped
with their lives. Thucydides sees the general abandonment of humane standards as the result of the teaching
not of the Sophists but of the war, which is, as he says, a
teacher, and a brutal teacher at that.

The Sophists have been saddled with more than their
fair share of the blame by the genius of a comic poet,
Aristophanes, and the still greater genius of a philosopher who, while claiming that books were deceivers and
that truth came only from the give-and-take of spoken
dialogue, wrote books of such brilliance, with such hyp-
notic grace, that he has imposed his own biased view of
fifth-century Athens on all succeeding generations. It
was Plato, of course, who made the word "Sophist" into
a term of abuse and also, though this aspect of his work
is seldom mentioned, tried to suppress the new humanities. It was perfectly logical that he should do so. They
had been created to provide education in citizenship for
that democracy which Plato loathed and despised, not
only because it had put his master Socrates to death but

also because he saw clearly the real flaws of Athenian imperial democracy—its inability to maintain a stable policy, its encouragement of sycophancy and political corruption; he saw also as flaws what were in fact its virtues—its openness to new ideas, its freedom of speech, its establishment of equality before the law. Plato's concern for truth and denunciation of the moral neutrality of much Sophistic teaching can only be praised, but in his search for a better form of education he threw out the baby with the bath water. In his ideal states, both the rigidly controlled nightmare of the *Republic* and the slightly less stifling bad dream of the *Laws,* the basic materials of the humanities, poetry, philosophy, history, and the arts are either expelled bag and baggage or else forced to sing an official song to please the censors. Plato is a great artist and philosopher, but there is surely no one reading this who would abandon even the most corrupt and inefficient democracy to live in his republic.

The training introduced by the Sophists obviously had its bad effects as well as its good ones; what system of education does not? But the good side of it has not been sufficiently emphasized. The Sophists trained their students to ask questions. This is a cardinal point seized on in Aristophanes' caricature of Sophistic education. When the old farmer Strepsiades gets back from the

thinking factory the son he has sent so that he can learn
the new technique and help his father get out of paying
his debts, he welcomes him, at first, with open arms.
"What a pleasure to see you back. Your whole counte-
nance says 'No!' You are all set to confront and confute,
and that 'What-did-you-say?' look we all know so well
is positively blooming on your face." There is truth in
this travesty; the Sophists encouraged their students to
question every received idea, to subject age-old concepts
of the relationship between man and god, man and society, to the criterion of reasoned, organized discussion. It
is in this period of Athenian history that we hear for the
first time doubts expressed about the value of aristocratic lineage, for example, and also about the superiority of Greeks to barbarians, for the first time discussion
of the position of women in society, of the nature of
political equality, and even of that sacrosanct, because
essential, institution of Greek life—slavery. Athenian
democracy, the first society we know of that was open to
the free play of ideas, was finding its voice in the new
education.

The educational controversy was reflected on the tragic
stage as well as the comic; in the *Philoctetes* of Sophocles, for example, but much more directly in a play by

Euripides, famous in its time but now extant only in fragments, the *Antiope*. This remarkable tragedy dealt with the mythical events which led to the founding of seven-gated Thebes. In the middle of a melodramatic plot typical of late Euripidean dramaturgy—two found-ling twins identify and rescue their mother, after which they tie her tormentor, a queen, to a wild bull to be dragged to death—the Athenian audience was treated to a debate for and against the new education. One of the twins, Zethus, urges the other, Amphion, to give up the life of music (the Greek word *mousike* embraces the idea of literature as well) and stick to practical realities. Ar-guing the virtues of the active life, on farm and battle-field, Zethus reproaches his brother for his lack of man-liness ("woman-like appearance") and inability to be of service to his friends in war and council. He accuses him of importing a muse who is "unsuitable, harmful, lazy, given to drink and spendthrift." The man, he says, who inherits a good livelihood but lets his household affairs go to waste and pursues pleasure in song will become remiss in both private and public duty and, for his friends, a nobody. "Take my advice," he tells his brother. "Put an end to your singing; practice the fair art of practical affairs; do what will win you a reputation as a man of sense. Dig, plow the earth, watch the flocks. Leave to others these elegant intellectual pursuits. . . ."

Amphion's reply defends the life of tranquillity, contemplation, and enjoyment. Life is unpredictable, a vacillation between happiness and misery; why not enjoy the good life while we can? But he goes farther and counters the claims Zethus made for the philistine in public life: "The quiet man is a source of salvation for his friends and a great benefit to his city." Amphion rejects the warlike aggressiveness characteristic of Zethus' speech. "Do not sing the praises of dangerous action. I have no liking for excessive boldness in a ship's captain, nor in a statesman either." But he ends by making a remarkable claim: "Your contempt for my lack of physical strength . . . is misplaced. If I can think straight, that is better than a powerful right arm. It is by a man's brains that cities are well governed and households too and in this lies great strength for war. . . ." It is Protagoras' claim: that intellectual training produces the good citizen.

We have to piece this dialogue together out of quotations by prose authors (chief among them Plato, who refers to it in the *Gorgias*), and we have no exact dramatic context for it. But the Roman poet Horace, more fortunate than we are, for he had the full text, tells us that Amphion lost the argument, yielded to his brother, and silenced his lyre (vase paintings which may show the influence of this famous play depict him hiding it under his cloak). This concession was a dramatic necessity, since the plot demanded that the two brothers proceed to rescue their mother, tie Dirce to a rampaging bull, and then lure the tyrant Lycus into a cave to his death. Amphion becomes the man of action, putting aside the lyre for the sword, and his success supports his claim; if in fact, as seems probable, Amphion is the speaker of the first lines on the papyrus fragment which has given us the ending of the play, he is the organizer and leader of the action which entraps the tyrant. But Lycus is not killed. Hermes, the god from the machine, appears to save his life, appoint Zethus and Amphion kings of the land in his stead, and order them to build the walls of Thebes.

Some twenty-five hundred years later Bertolt Brecht, a refugee in Denmark, wrote a poem which began, "Wer baute das siebentorige Theben?" "Who built seven-gated Thebes? In the books stand recorded the names of kings. Did the kings haul the broken rock?" Brecht does not have to tell us the answer to that question; it was, of course, the working class that built Thebes. And one might have expected that Euripides' Hermes would give the job to Zethus the practical hand, the rough diamond, the philistine. But the myth gave a different answer, and Euripides was happy to follow it. Exactly what task Hermes did assign to Zethus we cannot tell, for the papyrus at this point has a hole in it; in any case, the instructions to Zethus are brief. Not so the god's command to Amphion: "I command Amphion to arm his hand with the lyre and sing the gods' praises. Huge rocks shall follow you, spellbound by your music; trees shall leave their firm setting in mother earth, making an easy task for the mason's hand." That lyre which Amphion hid under his cloak is to be brought out in triumph; music and poetry will build the walls of Thebes.

IV

We have come all the way back to the birth of the humanities to find that they were on the defensive then as they are now, that, then as now, they were vulnerable to the accusation that they posed questions but gave no definitive answers, that their effect was often unsettling, if not subversive, that they made their devotees unfit for real life—"a mind unfinished," said Pindar, "and fed with scraps of a thousand virtues." But we have seen, too, that they came into being as an education for democracy, that in spite of their deficiencies and the inadequacy of some of their purveyors, they performed that function well, and found their defenders. The humanities are still today the vital core of an education for a democracy; the proof of that statement is furnished daily by democracy's enemies. Dictatorships cannot tolerate the humanities; for too many generations now we have watched the poets, novelists, dramatists, critics, philosophers, historians, and professors exiled, imprisoned, or murdered by totalitarian regimes.

For that group of studies we call the humanities came into being as an education for democracy, a training in free citizenship; all through its long history it has been the advocate of free thought and speech; it has flourished most brilliantly wherever those freedoms were respected and faced repression and banishment wherever they were not. And this is the strongest argument for the humanities today. Not that they will lead to positions of emolument—it is no longer true and was an ignoble argument to start with; not that they will make the individual life a richer, deeper experience—though this is true; but that they will prepare the young mind for the momentous choices, the critical decisions which face our world today.

The Greeks relegated practical skills, *techne,* to a lower sphere; the ideal of a free man was leisure, *schole,* and the pursuit of wisdom which it permitted. But the modern world has made *techne* into a prodigious instrument for scientific investigation and material progress—only to discover, not, we hope, too late, that it is also a monster which may destroy all life on the planet, instantaneously or by slow erosion of the environment, which by genetic engineering may create unpredictable and possibly dangerous forms of life, human and otherwise, which may develop mechanical brains superior in efficiency to our own—there is no end to the doomsday visions which haunt our dreams and come each day closer to fulfillment.

It will fall to the lot of today's younger generation to deal with these issues and others just as crucial, to take whatever action can be taken before time runs out. What action? Technology will not help here, for technology is part of the problem; the computer will not give the answer, for the question involves something that cannot be quantified—human values. What is a human being? What is the good life? The good society? What limits are there to individual loyalty to the state? To human exploitation of the universe? These questions and others like them are what the humanities have been asking ever since they first took shape in Athens. They are questions to which there is no simple answer, problems for which there is no neat solution—but one thing is certain. Those who have never looked beyond the edges of their technical fields or their business affairs to ask themselves what broader purpose, if any, is served by their activity, whose answer to the question "Why the next step?" is "Because it's there" are not as well equipped to chart a course for a free nation in the twenty-first century as those who, familiar by their studies with the best that has been thought or said, with the whole history of the human spirit, are painfully conscious of the frailty of all mortal structures, social, economic, and political, fully aware that, in A.E. Housman's words, "the troubles of our proud and angry dust / are from eternity and shall not fail," but equally aware that time and again in the long history of our race humanity, fired by leadership which translated into action moral, political, or social ideals, has shown itself capable of just the kind of intelligence and courage it will need if it is to survive in the dangerous years to come.

Three

THE CONTINUITY OF GREEK CULTURE

I

My title is obviously overambitious. The continuity of Greek culture is a vast and complex field of study, demanding of its practitioners expertise in ancient, Byzantine, and modern Greek language, literature, and history, in Slavic and Turkish language and history, in the ritual and theology of the Orthodox church, and a score of related disciplines, more in fact than one scholar can master in a lifetime. It is also an area of continuing interest and controversy. As recently as 1981, for example, the Hellenic Cultural Centre in London organized a panel discussion on the theme "3000 Years of Greek Identity." The three panels, chaired by the Byzantine scholar Robert Browning, were addressed by three Greeks brought up outside Greece, three Greeks raised in Greece, and three English scholars: one of the talks by Costa Carras, "3000 Years of Greek Identity—Myth or Reality?," was published in London in 1983. And it is a field in which fresh data are constantly supplied to feed fresh discussion.

Even in one narrow field, the continuity of the language, Professor Shipp, an Australian scholar who is a noted authority on the language of Homer, published a book entitled *Modern Greek Evidence for the Ancient Greek Vocabulary;* and in 1974 Nikolas Andriotis, working in the opposite direction, published in Vienna his *Lexikon der Archaismen in neugriechischen Dialekten.* Here indeed are to be found three thousand years, or more, of Greek identity. The language inscribed on the fire-baked clay tablets found at Pylos, on the mainland, and at Knossos, on Crete, dating from about 1600 B.C., is recognizably a primitive form of the language in which the newspapers of Athens are written today. Of course, in this immense stretch of time, the language has undergone many changes, but no other European language even comes close to claiming such a longevity; the only real parallel, in fact, is Chinese.

The profusion of studies published on this and all the other aspects of the long Greek tradition is such that any deluded writer who thinks he can build a bridge between ancient and modern Greece in a short essay will end up constructing a shaky structure at best and may find himself lamenting, like bridge builders in the famous medieval Greek ballad:

αλιμονο στους κοπους μας, κριμα στη δουλεψη μας
ολομερις να χτιζουμε, το βραδυ να γκρεμειεται

(Alas for our trouble, alas for our work,
To build it all day long, and have it collapse in the evening.)

I shall aim lower. What I will do is to write about my own encounter with modern Greece, its language and culture, the encounter of a classical literary scholar, brought up on Homer and Sophocles, with the Greece of Karamanlis and Papandreou (the elder Papandreou, I may add—I first went to Greece in 1958). I should begin by explaining that I grew up in England, where I learned ancient Greek at school in London and then went on to St. John's College in Cambridge to read classics in the early thirties of this century.

The training I received was rigidly linguistic in emphasis (and in that was quite typical). The method seemed to have been designed with an eye to producing scholars who could write near-perfect Platonic prose and correct (but dull) Sophoclean iambic verse. I went through three years of Cambridge with the general impression that all the Greek worth reading came to a full stop with Theocritus (though there was, of course, the New Testament, but *that* was something for people studying divinity) and furthermore that Greek history came to a stop with the death of Alexander the Great in 323 B.C. (after that it was Hellenistic history). Toward the end of my career at Cambridge I discovered that a friend of mine, who had chosen archaeology as his special field and was on his way to the British School in Athens, was studying, from a German handbook (there wasn't one in English), modern Greek. After talking to him and looking at the book, I asked my tutor whether perhaps an acquaintance with modern Greek might be useful. "Not only will it not be useful," he said, "—the only people who use it are archaeologists who have to go there—not only will it not be useful; it will corrupt your prose style, and you will end up writing Greek that sounds like Polybius."

This Olympian disdain for people who actually went to modern Greece and who didn't *have* to go there was no new thing: in the spring of 1877 Oscar Wilde, then an undergraduate reading Greats at Magdalen College, Oxford, went on a trip to Greece with Professor Mahaffy of his former college, Trinity College, Dublin; they saw the excavations at Olympia, the temple at Bassae, Argos, Aegina, and Athens. Unfortunately for Wilde, he got back to Oxford three weeks late for the beginning of term (there were no jets in those days). "Voyages to Greece," says his biographer Richard Ellmann, "were not common in the seventies of the last century. That they were necessary to a classical course in Oxford was more than Magdalen was ready to concede." Wilde was temporarily suspended for the rest of the academic year and deprived of his scholarship money. "I was sent down from Oxford," he said later, "for being the first undergraduate to visit Olympia."

This attitude, however, was not confined to the English classical establishment. Sometime in the early sixties of this century I asked a French archaeologist who had spent most of his life in Greece at the Ecole Française whether he read the modern Greek poets. (I had just discovered, with immense excitement, the poetry of

Cavafy and Seferis.) "No," he said, "I have to know enough modern Greek to talk to the workmen on the dig, but I try to keep my acquaintance with it to a minimum—it might spoil my appreciation of the subtleties of Plato's style."

And I am sorry to say that this attitude toward modern Greek and modern Greece, typical of so many scholars, especially those concerned with literature, was just as prevalent in the United States when I first began to do graduate work and then to teach at Yale after the Second World War. My colleagues spent their summers and their sabbatical years in London, Paris, Vienna, Rome—cities where there were manuscripts of ancient Greek authors to collate, where the great libraries offered immense bibliographical resources, the great cities their comforts and cultural amenities, and the universities their classical scholars for consultation and discussion. I, too, when my first fellowship allowed me to travel, in 1953, went to Rome and Florence, partly because, as a result of military service in Italy in the Second World War, I spoke Italian, but also because in Florence the Biblioteca Laurenziana held the great manuscript of Sophocles, on whom I was working at the time. Greece was a place to visit, perhaps, but not to stay in (like New York); those scholars who did go contented themselves with a visit to the most important classical sites. They returned to their universities not so much disillusioned (for they had expected very little) as confirmed in their conviction that between the Greece of Pericles and Sophocles on the one hand and that of Venizelos and Seferis on the other (not that they knew very much about either of these two) there was a gap so wide that little or nothing of value to the classicist was to be learned from a closer knowledge of the life, literature, and language of modern Greece.

To the Greeks themselves, whose early training and later study reinforced their consciousness of the continuity of the Greek tradition, such an attitude must appear bizarre, just as it would appear strange to Englishmen if a foreign scholar of Chaucer or Shakespeare found nothing useful for his studies in the language and customs of modern England. But this attitude exists and persists, and since I too shared it to some extent before I had the good fortune to spend a whole year in Greece I would like to describe it and try to explain it. I have long since been free of it, but the converted heretic is perhaps the most competent authority on the beliefs he has rejected.

■ ■ ■

II

To begin with, there is the look of the place. No one can fail to be overwhelmed by the beauty and mystery of the Altis at Olympia by moonlight, or of Delphi at any hour (any hour, that is, when there are not ten thousand tourists taking pictures), and no one can fail to be impressed by the huge yet delicate beauty of the theater at Epidaurus, the long gallery in the fortress at Tiryns, the splendid yet somehow haunted site of Agamemnon's palace at Mycenae, and the tomb of the Athenian and Plataean dead on the plain where "Marathon looks on the sea." But these are secluded ancient sites, where the scholar can easily imagine himself in the Greece of classical or archaic times. The rest of Greece, however, is another kettle of fish. The scholar of Greek literature who manages to find his way behind the Larisa Station to what was Kolonos Hippios, with the marvelous lines of Sophocles ringing in his ears,

> ευιππου ξενε, τασδε χωρας
> ικου τα κρατιστα γας επαυλα,
> τον αργητα Κολωνον, ενθ'
> α λιγεια μινυρεται
> . . . αηδων . . .
> (*Oedipus at Colonus,* lines 668ff.)

> (Stranger, you have come to the land of fine
> horses, to earth's fairest home, white Colonus,
> where the nightingale, a permanent guest,
> trills her clear notes in green glades, amid the
> wine-dark ivy in the gods' sacred wood, heavy
> with fruit and berries, shaded from the sun,
> shielded from wind and weather.)

is in for a terrible shock; what he will find at the end of
the bus ride has little to do with horses and still less to
do with nightingales. And suppose he tries to follow
Socrates and Phaedrus out to the shady spot where they
talked by the river Ilissos.

> This plane tree is spreading and tall [says
> Plato's Socrates] and there is a lovely shade
> from the high branches of the agnus; now that
> it is in full flower, it will make the place fra-
> grant. And what a lovely stream under the
> plane tree! and how cool to the feet . . . and the
> freshness of the air and the shrill summery
> music of the cicadas. And as a crowning de-
> light this grass, thick on the gentle slope, just
> right to rest your head on it most comfortably.

Our scholar will be a very clever man if he can find the
Ilissos at all and a very disappointed one if he does.

Reluctantly, dodging traffic at every intersection, he makes his way back to the Acropolis, where, even though it is scarred and broken, there is enough left of the Parthenon and the Propylaea to remind him of the glories of Periclean Athens.

Outside Athens things are not much better. Our scholar's first view of Salamis and the straits in which the Greek fleet, watched by Xerxes from his throne, routed and sank the Persian galleys, will probably include the rusting hulks lying at anchor off Skaramangas; and all the way to the site of the Eleusinian Mysteries at Eleusis he will have to look at the plume of white smoke from the huge Herakles cement factory. Where are the pine trees on the Theban mountains, the haunts of Dionysos and his maenads, of nymphs and satyrs? Where is the narrow pass that Leonidas and his three hundred Spartans held against the Persian hordes? (It would take an army corps to hold it now.) Where are the bees of Hymettos? The birds of Aristophanes? The seven gates of Thebes? Only in the books the scholar knows so well and to which he returns with relief. The first impressions of modern Greece, and particularly Athens, are enough to convince most scholars that they will understand the culture and literature of the fifth century B.C. much better working in a study in Oxford or New Haven than they ever will sitting in a *kafeneion* near

Plateia tis Omonoias or riding the bus to Levadia.

Then there are the people, the Greeks themselves. To the visiting scholar they are the kindest and most solicitous of hosts (particularly in the country, where their hospitality can be overwhelming), hardworking, honest, and admirable people; but, thinks the scholar, they don't *look* like the ancient Greeks. He has come to Greece for the first time with the idealized faces of the young men on the Parthenon frieze stamped on his memory, his mind full of Homeric tags like *xanthos Menelaos,* a phrase which, particularly if he is of Anglo-Saxon or Germanic stock, he has been taught to translate "blond Menelaos." In Athens he finds himself in a world of men and women who seem to be a startling contrast to the ideal faces that have haunted the imagination since he first saw them in the British Museum— of people who bear no resemblance to the gods and goddesses whose exquisitely proportioned features, set in the eternity of marble gilded by time, first drew him to his lifelong study of Greek.

And finally there is the language. He knows that it has changed somewhat in twenty-five hundred years but still feels a certain confidence. After all, he has often successfully plowed his way through scholarly articles in modern Greek and occasionally read with some understanding a Greek newspaper bought in New York or London.

Armed with his many years of study of ancient Greek and perhaps a few days on the boat devoted to a modern Greek phrase book, he expects to be able to manage fairly well when he gets there; after all, he has been studying Greek all his life. But the first contact with spoken Greek, especially if the speaker is a Piraeus taxi driver, can be a shattering experience. The visiting professor is reduced, like all his ignorant fellow passengers, to conducting his negotiations for a ride to Athens in what passes among Piraeus taxi drivers for English. Later, after buying a grammar and making a serious stab at the language, he begins to make some progress, but he realizes with growing despair that the reason he could read the scholarly articles and newspapers is that they are written in a Greek that tries to preserve as much of the ancient language as possible, whereas the waiters and bus drivers and policemen with whom he has to deal on his travels seem to be talking a different language. Modern Greek seems to have so little connection with the language of Demosthenes (Good Lord, it hasn't even got an *infinitive*) that he sees no point in trying to learn it.

On my first visit to Greece, once comfortably ensconced in a hotel in Iannina (we had arrived on a ferry from Brindisi to Igoumenitsa), I displayed my knowledge of Greek by translating the headlines of the newspaper to my wife. But the balloon was soon punctured when she said, "Since you seem to know the language so well, why don't you call up and get us two more pillows and one more towel?" The language of Sophocles and Aristophanes was no help: my best effort—*pherete mou ena linon kai duo proskephalaia*—was answered by a series of excited questions that, unfortunately, I could not understand, and I was reduced to the expedient of going down to the desk and using sign language.

III

These first impressions are, of course, my own; but I am sure, from comparing notes with colleagues, that they are fairly representative. But not many scholars of ancient Greek literature have the opportunity that was offered to me—to stay on for a whole year and find that these first impressions, like most first impressions, were unreliable.

First, the land itself. It is true that the country has changed enormously since the fifth century, but we forget that many of the things we complain of were already a cause for concern in ancient times—deforestation, for example. In Plato's dialogue the *Critias,* the Athenian aristocrat after whom the dialogue is named draws a nostalgic contrast between present and past:

> What now remains compared with what existed then is like the skeleton of a sick man, all the fat and soft earth wasted away and only the bare framework of the land left. . . . The country was once unspoiled: its mountains were arable highlands and what is now stony fields was once good soil. And the earth was enriched by the annual rains which were not lost as now by flowing from the bare land into the sea . . . but deep soil received and stored the water . . . there were forests on the mountains; there are some which now have nothing but food for bees that had trees not so very long ago and the rafters from those that were chopped down to roof the large buildings are still sound.

And there are many features of Greek soil and climate that have never changed: the weather, for example. One has to live through a Greek summer to know why Pindar began his first Olympian ode with the bald statement *Ariston men hudor,* "Water is best." I first read that line in England, where water is so plentiful that sometimes there doesn't seem to be anything else (someone once suggested that Thales, with his theory that all things are water, must have spent some time in England), and the line didn't seem to make much sense. (Some schoolboy wit had, in fact, proposed a correction to the text in my book, *zythos* for *hudor,* to produce the meaning "Beer is best.") It is only in Greece that one feels the true force of that magnificent opening phrase, when one has come, like the Greeks themselves, to prefer a glass of water in the heat to beer or lemonade or wine, to call, at the *kafeneion,* for more and more *neraiki;* only a Greek summer and the total dehydration two hours in the sun can produce will make one feel the full force of Pindar's words. But this is only one small example. One has to experience a Greek thunderstorm, with the lightning visible for miles and the thunder crash echoing from mountain to mountain through the clear air, to feel the terror and majesty of the last scenes of the *Oedipus at Colonus,* to know what is meant by the thunderbolt Zeus brandishes with his right arm. And the sea does not change. Standing on the Acropolis looking down on the gulf at sunset, one can see what look like wide tracks in the pattern of rough sea and smooth; they are surely Homer's "paths of the sea" *(hygra keleutha).* And one has to walk the bare Attic hills in the spring and see the incredible carpet of richly colored wildflowers springing from barren rock to understand why Pindar called Athens "violet crowned." With time, as the seasons change, as the olives are shaken from the trees, gathered, and pressed, as the soil is plowed and sown, as much later the fruit begins to ripen and fall, as the grain is winnowed on the high circular threshing floor that must be the origin of the orchestra in which the tragic chorus danced, the scholar who has had the good fortune to spend a whole year in Greece can learn to feel the rhythm of the Greek seasons, of the Greek earth, a rhythm unlike that of his own country and one that has not changed since Hesiod wrote its rulebook and its praise.

So much for the land, but what of the people? The initial disappointment most Greek scholars feel when confronted for the first time by modern Greeks en masse is due solely to the illusions they bring with them. England and Germany were the two great centers of Greek studies in the nineteenth century, and both nations created a vision of the ancient Greeks that had more to do with their ideal of themselves than with reality. In this misconception they were encouraged by the fact that ancient Greek art was known to the nineteenth century mainly in the form of sculpture; Attic vases, which came mostly from Etruscan tombs, were labeled "Etruscan" until late in the century. And sculpture, at any rate the unpainted marble of the Parthenon frieze, allows the beholder to clothe its reticent surface in any colors he pleases. "If horses had gods they would look like horses," Xenophanes blandly observed long ago; and one has only to turn to the trashiest kind of English and American novels—the surest evidence of a people's deep-seated prejudices and most widely accepted clichés—to find what image of the ancient Greeks was formed in the Western mind. In such novels the hero is described, as often as not, as looking "like a Greek god." Investigation of the text generally reveals that he is a little over six feet tall and has blue eyes and pale golden hair. He looks, in fact, exactly like the Edwardian ideal of the Oxford undergraduate. No wonder the first sight of the crowds in Piraeus by day and Omonoia by night gives the Western classicist a jolt!

There is really no reason why it should. The vases with their black-haired and black-bearded figures and, still more, the painted archaic sculpture in the Acropolis museum give a picture of ancient Greeks who look startlingly like the modern article. There is one *kore* in that museum, with black abundant hair and dark, wide eyes, whose modern sisters can be seen any day of the week

walking down Hodos Stadiou. And in any case, the ancient literature gives no basis for this Western feeling
(subliminal, but therefore all the stronger) that ancient
Greeks were tall, blond, and blue-eyed. "Xanthos
Menelaos" *may* have been blond, though the word more
likely means red- or brown-haired, but surely the fact
that he is so often called "xanthos" suggests that the
other Achaian chieftains were not. And in Sophocles'
Antigone, when the chorus wants to say "ever since I
became an old man," they say "ever since my hair
changed from *black* to white,"

> . . . εξ οτου λευκην εγω
> τηνδ' εκ μελαινης αμφιβαλλομαι τριχα
> (lines 1091ff.)

It is, of course, not only in his looks that the modern
Greek resembles his ancestors. The men sitting in the
kafeneion discussing the latest rumors and playing inter-
minable games of *tavli* are no different from the men
sitting by the fountain in Corinth playing *pessoi* (it
seems to have been almost exactly the same game) from
whom the *paedagogos* in Euripides' *Medea* picked up
the rumor that his mistress was to be banished. The
ancient Greeks were famous racers, especially in chari-
ots; anyone who is about to take his first taxi ride in

central Athens would do well to prepare himself psycho-
logically by reading the description of the chariot race in
Sophocles' *Electra*. I once thought of writing a Pindaric
ode in praise of a driver who got me through rush-hour
traffic to the station mainly by driving on the sidewalks.
To strike a more serious note, the same touchy sense of
personal honor that is at the root of Achilles' wrath still
governs relations between man and man in modern
Greece; Greek society still fosters in the individual a
fierce sense of his privileges, no matter how small, of his
rights, no matter how confined, of his personal worth,
no matter how low. And to defend it, he will stop, like
Achilles, at nothing. Even its name is still the same,
filotimo, filotimia. And on the larger scale of national
politics, little has changed; modern Greek politics has no
better analyst than Thucydides, whose somber description of Athens in the last decades of the fifth century B.C.
reads like a foreshadowing of the tragic events of 1940–
50. The more one lives in modern Greece, the more one
is forced to see the modern in the light of the ancient and
also to reread the ancient Greeks with new insights
drawn from a knowledge of the modern.

And finally, the language. It is in some ways the most
rewarding aspect of modern Greece for the classical

scholar. A closer study of the spoken language reveals an intimate and live relationship between the languages of fifth- and twentieth-century Athens. Not only can the modern spoken language be called on to elucidate obscure words in ancient authors, as has been brilliantly done in some passages of Aristophanes, but also the scholar who learned his Greek as a dead language has in modern Greece the exhilarating experience of finding it alive: he can hear in the *laiki*, the open-air market, near Kolonaki, every Friday the very tone of Aristophanes' sausage seller and market women and on the docks of Piraeus the sharp wit and banter of the sailors who manned the great fleets which set out from what is now Passalimani.

All the scholar has to do is to forget the artificial *katharevousa* of the newspaper editorials and government bureaucracy and listen to and learn from the popular speech of Greece, which is also, of course, the base from which the poets work. I ran up against the difficulties involved in the "language question" halfway through my year in Greece, which was 1960–61.

I had already been appointed director of Harvard's Center for Hellenic Studies, in Washington, but had not yet taken up its responsibilities. Professor Bakalakis of the University of Thessaloniki had somehow heard about the center and also tracked me down (I was keeping away from academic circles so that I could get some work done); he invited me to come to Thessaloniki to make a speech explaining what the center was. It was a good opportunity to try out my newly learned modern Greek and also perhaps to recruit some Greek fellows for the center (and in fact over the next twenty years no fewer than five young scholars came from Thessaloniki to spend a year at the center). I accepted and started to work on my speech.

On the overnight train going up to Saloniki I suddenly got cold feet. There I was, going to speak in the *dimotiki* I had learned talking to ordinary Athenians, to an academic audience on an academic subject. They might well think it, coming from a foreigner, presumptuous, even insulting. At the last stop before Thessaloniki— Larissa, I think it was—I bought a whole clutch of newspapers and with the help of the editorials rewrote the speech in flowing *katharevousa*.

Next morning, at seven o'clock, we arrived. I had an appointment with Linos Politis at ten, so I walked around the town, especially along the magnificent seafront. My bag, however, was getting to be a nuisance; I happened to see the office of the American Express, went in and explained my situation, and asked if they could keep the bag for me, which, very courteously, they agreed to do.

Six or seven hours later, after a fascinating interview with Linos Politis, and a magnificent lunch in a restaurant on the waterfront, I was to be taken to my hotel for a rest before the speech and asked my host to stop by the American Express. To my horror, here was a big sign on the door: ΚΛΕΙΣΤΟ. What's more, it wasn't going to open again until six—too late for me. The speech was due at five-thirty. So, once at the hotel, instead of a rest, I had to recompose the speech, in double-quick time, and this time there was no fooling around with the *katharevousa*.

The speech went off well. I had inserted two jokes to test the audience's comprehension of my imperfect accent—and the students laughed at both places. Afterwards at dinner, I told Politis what had happened. For a moment I thought he look shocked and that I had made a mistake to tell him, but then he began to laugh. He laughed very loudly and went on laughing. And finally he said to me, "Your lucky *daimon* was at work. Leaving that second version at American Express was the best thing you could have done." And he proceeded to explain that Thessaloniki was, so to speak, the home and champion of *demotiki,* was writing its grammar and syntax—"If you had tried your warmed-up *katharevousa* on the audience, they would have tried hard not to laugh." I told him that I had been suddenly terrified by the memory of a professor of law at the University of Athens who had dominated an Athenian dinner party with long discussions in a very high-flying *katharevousa;* he had been told I was a professor of ancient Greek and informed me that when he went to Munich the German professor there told him he spoke like Plato. "Oh," said Politis, in a tone of good-humored patience. "Athens . . ."

Even this distinction between an official quasi-literary language and popular speech goes back to antiquity; we still have handbooks written in the Roman imperial period that specify lists of acceptable "Attic" words and rule out others. And we know, from the private letters that have emerged, written on papyrus, from the sands of Egypt, that Greeks there in the second century were speaking a Greek that had sometimes startling resemblances to the modern language. A boy's letter to his father, for example, in which the child asks to be taken along on a trip to Alexandria, begins, exactly as a modern schoolboy might begin: *Lipon, pater mou* . . . "Well, father . . ." Not only is the word *loipon* (as it was spelled in fifth-century Athens and still is) used in its modern sense of "Well . . ."; the boy's phonetic spelling shows that the itacism which is such a pronounced feature of the modern language had already begun.

"It is strange," says George Thomson in his brilliant

book *The Greek Language,* "that so many scholars visiting Greece to refresh themselves at the fount of Hellenism should spend all their time contemplating the material remains of antiquity without realizing that the object of their quest still flows from the lips of the people." In this aspect of modern Greece are great treasures of new insight and fresh understanding ready for the classical scholar to discover, and without the pains of excavation. All he has to do is learn and listen. And also read, for the great poets of modern Greece—and Western Europe is slowly realizing that they are among the world's greatest poets, Cavafy, Seferis, Sikelianos, Elytis,—all of them are heirs to the legacy of ancient Greece, which is both a blessing and a burden; all of them draw strength from the tradition even as they try to maintain their independence of it.

What modern Greece offers the student of classical literature and thought is just as great as what it offers the archaeologist, if not greater. It can renew and refresh his contact with the ancient sources in hundreds of ways. Above all, he can ground in Greek earth that *Nephelokykyggia* (cloud-cuckoo Land), the "ideal" Greece he has conjured up from books; it will enable him at last "to give to airy nothing a local habitation and a name."

NOTES ON SOURCES

Foreword

Richard Porson of Cambridge (p. 14) was one of the greatest English Greek scholars; he was also a mordant wit and an incurable alcoholic. His account of his visit to two famous Greek scholars in Germany runs:

■   ■   ■

> *I went to Frankfort, and got drunk*
> *With that most learn'd professor Brunck;*
> *I went to Worms, and got more drunken*
> *With that more learn'd professor Ruhncken.*

The ten plays of Euripides (p. 15) were augmented by nine more plays discovered toward the end of the Byzantine era, bringing the total to nineteen, though one of them, the *Rhesus,* is generally attributed to a later poet.

The statement by Thucydides (pp. 19–20) is from the *History,* 1.70.9.

The remark by Horace (p. 22) reads, in the Latin original, *Naturam expelles furca, tamen usque recurret* (*Epistles,* 1.10.24).

1   The Oldest Dead White European Males

Frank Turner's *The Greek Heritage in Victorian Britain* (p. 27) was published by Yale University Press (New Haven, 1981).

"Autumn Journal" (pp. 29–30) is from MacNeice's *Collected Poems,* ed. E. R. Dodds (New York: Oxford University Press, 1967).

The passage cited by Pierre Vidal-Naquet (p. 35) can be found in his *The Black Hunter* (Baltimore: Johns Hopkins University Press, 1986).

Louis Gernet's *Anthropologie de la Grèce antique*

(p. 35) was published in English as *The Anthropology of Ancient Greece* (Baltimore: Johns Hopkins University Press, 1981).

The books of Jean-Pierre Vernant (p. 35) include *The Origins of Greek Thought* (Ithaca: Cornell University Press, 1962); *Myth and Thought among the Greeks* (London: Routledge & Kegan Paul, 1983); and, in collaboration with Vidal-Naquet, *Myth and Tragedy in Ancient Greece* (New York: Zone Books, 1988).

Marcel Detienne's *Les Jardins d'Adonis* (p. 36) was published in English as *The Gardens of Adonis* (Hassocks: Harvester Press, 1977).

Pierre Vidal-Naquet's *Atlas historique* (p. 36) was published by Hachette (Paris, 1987).

La Cuisine du sacrifice grec (p. 36) was published in English as *The Cuisine of Sacrifice among the Greeks* (Chicago: University of Chicago Press, 1989).

Walter Burkert's *Homo Necans* (p. 36) was published by the University of California Press (Berkeley, 1983).

Bruno Snell's *The Discovery of the Mind* (pp. 37–38) was published by Harvard University Press (Cambridge, 1953) and Harper and Row (New York, 1960).

The American scholar alluded to on p. 40 is Eric Havelock; his argument can be found in *Preface to Plato* (Cambridge: Harvard University Press, 1963; New York: Grosset and Dunlap, 1967), pp. 81–84, 120–22.

For more on Snell's dismissal of *demas* (p. 43), see Bernard Knox, "The Human Figure in Homer," in *New*

Perspectives in Early Greek Art, ed. Diana Buitron-Oliver (Washington, D.C.: National Gallery of Art, 1991), pp. 93–96.

The quotation by Albin Lesky (p. 44) is from *Greek Tragedy* (London: Ernest Benn, 1963), p. 124.

M. I. Finley's remarks on slavery (p. 47) are from *Ancient Slavery and Modern Ideology* (New York: Viking, 1980), pp. 57, 65.

The lines from Aristophanes' *Lysistrata* (p. 51) are translated by Douglass Parker, in *Aristophanes: Four Comedies,* ed. William Arrowsmith (Ann Arbor: University of Michigan Press, 1969).

Eva Keuls's *The Reign of the Phallus* (p. 52) was published by Harper and Row (New York, 1985).

The lines from Aristophanes' *Frogs* (pp. 56–57) are translated by Richmond Lattimore, in *Aristophanes: Four Comedies.*

Nothing to Do with Dionysos?, ed. John J. Winkler and Froma Zeitlin (p. 57) was published by Princeton University Press (Princeton, 1990).

Seamus Heaney's version of Sophocles' *Philoctetes* (pp. 62–63) was published as *The Cure at Troy* (New York: Farrar, Straus and Giroux, 1991).

2   The Walls of Thebes

The advice by Thomas Gaisford (pp. 72–73) is from W. Tuckwell, *Reminiscences of Oxford,* 2d ed. (London: Smith, Elder, 1907), p. 124.

The verses on pp. 74 and 75–77 are from Louis MacNeice's "Autumn Journal," in *The Collected Poems of Louis MacNeice,* ed. E. R. Dodds (New York: Oxford University Press, 1967).

Matthew Arnold's definition of "culture" (pp. 75–76) is from *Literature and Dogma* (preface to the edition of 1873); the second quotation is from his poem "Dover Beach"; Arnold's division of England into barbarians, philistines, and "Populace" can be found in his preface to *Culture and Anarchy* (1869).

Copleston's argument (p. 76) is quoted by Richard Jenkyns in *The Victorians and Ancient Greece* (Cambridge: Harvard University Press, 1980), p. 60.

The funeral eulogy for a Roman aristocrat (p. 80) is from Pliny the Elder's *Natural History* 7.139–40.

The passages from Horace (pp. 80–81) are *Epistles,* 2.103ff. and 156ff.

Cato's "aversion to philosophy" (p. 81) is mentioned in Plutarch, *Marcus Cato,* chap. 23.

Cicero's comment on the statues (p. 82) is from his *In Verrem,* 4.3.

Cicero's defense of literature and the liberal arts (pp. 82–86) is from his *Pro Archia,* 2.3.14–16.

The statements by Pindar (pp. 88–89) are from *Pythian,* 2.86; *Nemean,* 3.42ff.; and *Nemean,* 3.40.

Athena's phrase (pp. 89–90) is from Aeschylus, *Eumenides,* 970.

The sentence by Plato (p. 94) is from *Protagoras,* 339A; Prodicus' method as the target of Plato's satire

(p. 95) is from the same dialogue, 337A–C; and Protagoras' response to Socrates (p. 96) is from 319A.

Thucydides' discussion of the plague of 430–427 B.C. (p. 97) can be found in the *History*, 2.53; his argument that war is a brutal teacher (p. 95) is from the *History*, 3.82.

The caricature by Aristophanes (pp. 98–99) is from the *Clouds*, 1172–74.

Horace tells us that Amphion lost the argument with Zethus (pp. 101–02) in his *Epistles*, 1.18.41ff.

The quotation from Euripides' *Antiope* (p. 103) is from Denys Page, *Greek Literary Papyri* (Cambridge: Loeb Classical Library, 1942), pp. 60–71.

3   The Continuity of Greek Culture

The remark by Oscar Wilde (p. 111) is from Richard Ellmann, *Oscar Wilde* (New York: Knopf, 1988), pp. 77–78.

The description of the shady spot by the river Ilissos where Socrates and Phaedrus talked (p. 115) is from Plato's *Phaedrus*, 230B–C.

The contrast between present and past (p. 120) is from Plato's *Critias*, 111B–C.

The text of the second-century letter from a boy to his father (p. 129) is from George D. Thomson, *The Greek Language* (Cambridge: Heffer, 1960), p. 47, no. 20.

INDEX